AF440879

Windows PowerShell and Scripting for Beginners

Complete Beginners Guide to learn Windows PowerShell and its Scripting

By

David Coding

© **Copyright 2020 by David Coding - All rights reserved.**

This document is geared towards providing exact and reliable information in regards to the topic and issue covered. The publication is sold with the idea that the publisher is not required to render accounting, officially permitted, or otherwise, qualified services. If advice is necessary, legal or professional, a practiced individual in the profession should be ordered.

- From a Declaration of Principles which was accepted and approved equally by a Committee of the American Bar Association and a Committee of Publishers and Associations.

In no way is it legal to reproduce, duplicate, or transmit any part of this document in either electronic means or in printed format. Recording of this publication is strictly prohibited and any storage of this document is not allowed unless with written permission from the publisher. All rights reserved.

The information provided herein is stated to be truthful and consistent, in that any liability, in terms of inattention or otherwise, by any usage or abuse of any policies, processes, or directions contained within is the solitary and utter responsibility of the recipient reader. Under no circumstances will any legal responsibility or blame be held against the publisher for any reparation, damages, or monetary loss due to the information herein, either directly or indirectly.

Respective authors own all copyrights not held by the publisher.

The information herein is offered for informational purposes solely, and is universal as so. The presentation of the information is without contract or any type of guarantee assurance.

The trademarks that are used are without any consent, and the publication of the trademark is without permission or backing by the trademark owner. All trademarks and brands within this book are for clarifying purposes only and are the owned by the owners themselves, not affiliated with this document.

Table of Contents

Introduction

Windows PowerShell is a standard tool for Windows and its administrators. It's a component of Microsoft Engineering Criteria (MECC), PowerShell management hooks are developed into server-based products, including Exchange, SharePoint, Microsoft SQL Server, and System Center.

This book offers a solid footing for the Info Tech professionals trying to come up to speed on this essential management technology for windows.

Reading this Guide

This guide exists to help Info Tech pros come up to speed quickly on the new Windows PowerShell. This guide is specifically aimed at several audiences, such as:

- Anyone who wants to be a professional in automating the day-to-day management of .NET networks or Windows.

- Anyone who wants to automate the installation and configuration of Microsoft .NET networking components.

- Anyone who wants to obtain configurability of their Windows machines and maximum power, either at home or in an unmanaged desktop workplace environment.

- Anyone who wants information on configure settings of Windows based machines.

Various sections of Windows PowerShell, cover a wide range of technologies. Depending on your needs and your current understanding of Microsoft tools, you might want to be focused on different areas of the concerned book.

System Requirements for PowerShell

You will need the following software and hardware to execute the exercises mentioned in this guide:

- Windows 7 or above, Windows Server R2 2012

- Server R2 2008, or Windows Server 2008 with Service Pack 2.

- A computer, having 1.6 GHz or a better processor (recommendation is 2 GHz)

- 2 GB RAM 64-bit

- Hard disk space, upto 4 GB

- Hard drive 5400 RPM

- A capable graphic card working at 1024 x 768 or higher display.

- A good Internet connection.

Depending upon your Windows configuration, you may require some Local Administrator rights to execute certain commands.

Scripts

Many of the chapters in this guide contains exercises that simply allows you to interactively try out some new material learned in the main text. Simplest way to download the scripts is to get it from this page:

http://aka.ms/PS3E/files/

You need to follow the instructions and you have to download the

PS3E_675117_Scripts.zip

Installing Scripts

After downloading, simply follow these steps to install the scripts on your desktop so that you may use them with the examples, mentioned in this guide.

1.   Unzip the PS3E_675117_Scripts.zip file that you downloaded from the book's website.

2.   Review the user license agreement. If you are fine with the terms and conditions, press NEXT.

Chapter 1: Fundamentals of Windows PowerShell

The release of Windows PowerShell continues to offer the real power to the network administrators. It combines the power of a scripting language to the unique command-line utilities, Windows Management Instrumentation, and even Microsoft Visual Basic, Windows PowerShell provides real ease. Implementation of thousands of cmdlets and advanced functions provides a vibrant ecosystem that provides a single line of easy-to-read commad-line code. In other words, you may say, PowerShell is the management solution for the Windows platform.

1.1 Existing Tools, Scripts, and Programs

In some aspects, it is a replacement for CMD (command-line shell). Basically, on Windows OS-based Desktops or Server Core executing, it is possible to replace the command-line shell with the PowerShell so that when the server starts up, it uses the PowerShell as the basic interface. After PowerShell launches, you may use a command-line to change the working directory, and then use dir. to produce a directory listing in the same way you would perform these tasks from the CMD shell.

>>> PS C:\Windows\System32> cd\

>>> PS C:\> dir

>>> Directory: C:\

>>> PS C:\>

You may also combine traditional command-line interpreter commands with other utilities, such as fsutil. This is shown here.

>>> PS C:\> md c:\test

>>> Directory: C:\

>>> PS C:\ > fsutil file createnew

>>> c:\test\myfile.txt 2000

>>> File c:\test\myfile.txt is created

>>> PS C:\ > cd c:\test

>>> PS C:\test> dir

>>> Directory: C:\test

>>> PS C:\test>

These two examples show PowerShell being used in any interactive way.

Interactivity is the key features of PowerShell, and you may use the PowerShell interactively, simply, by opening a PowerShell prompt and entering some commands. You may enter the commands one at a time, or you can group them like an archieved file.

Use of "cmdlets", aka. Commandlets

While using Windows console applications and built-in command-lines, you may also use the "cmdlets", aka., commandlets. Commandlets are built into PowerShell. Moreover, they may be developed by any developer. The Windows PowerShell team creates the core commandlets, but many teams at Microsoft were involved in creating the thousands of commandlets that were included with the latest version of Windows, aka. Windows 10. Commandlets are some executable files, but commandlets take some advantage of facilities built into PowerShell so they are easy to develop and execute.

Commandlets are not the scripts, that are not compiled codes, because they are developed using a special .NET Framework. Moreover, PowerShell comes with about 1,350 commandlets for Windows blue and Windows 10, and as some additional feature and additional roles are applied, so are additional commandlets. These commandlets are developed to assist the administrator and network or consultant to take advantage of the power of the Windows PowerShell without knowing any scripting language or script programming. One of the basic advantages of the PowerShell is that commandlets use a standardized naming convention that allows you to follow a verb-noun sequence, for example, Get-Process, Get-EventLog, or Get-Help. The commandlets that uses the verb display info about the item on the right side of your dash. The commandlets that use the set verb modifies or sets the information about the items on the right side of your dash, as well. Example of a commandlet that uses the set-verb is known as Set-Service, this may be used to change the mode of starting a service. All the commandlets use one of the standard verb type words or phrases. To find a list of the verbs, you may use the commandlet Get-Verb. In Windows PowerShell, there are nearly 100 approved verbs.

1.2 Installing the latest version of Windows PowerShell

The Windows PowerShell comes with the Windows 10 Client. You may download the Windows Framework 5.0 Management package, it contains some updated versions for the WMI, Windows PowerShell 5.0, and Windows Remote Management from the Microsoft Center. Additionally, Windows 10 also comes with built-in Windows PowerShell 5.0, so, there is no Management Windows Framework package available for download.

Deploying the Windows PowerShell to down level OS

When you download the Windows PowerShell from this source:

http://www.microsoft.com/downloads

You may deploy it to your enterprise by using these standard methods.

Here are some methods that you may use to set up the deployment of Windows PowerShell:

- You have to create a group policy object in active directory domain services (AD DS) and link it to the appropriate OU.

- Now, you have to create a Microsoft systems center configuration manager package and advertise it to the appropriate organizational unit or collection.

- Now, add the windows management framework packages to a central file share or webpage for self-service.

- Now, approve the update in software update services, when available.

If you aren't deploying an entire enterprise, the easiest manner to install the PowerShell is to download the package and set it up through the wizard.

Using the Command-Line Utilities

Command-line utilities can be used directly within the Windows PowerShell, as explained earlier. The Windows PowerShell pipelining and formatting features are the pro of using command-line utilities in the PowerShell, as opposed to running them in the command-line prompt interpreter. Furthermore, if you have batch files or CMD files already using existing command-line prompt utilities, you may easily modify them to run within the Windows PowerShell environment.

The following procedure illustrates how ipconfig commands are added to a text file.

1.   Start Windows PowerShell by choosing Start, then go to Run and then type PowerShell. The Windows prompt of the PowerShell will open by default at the root of the user folder.

2.   Now, type the command ipconfig and execute it.

>>> PS C:\> ipconfig /all

3.   Now, pipeline the results of ipconfig to the text file. This is shown here.

>>> PS C:\> ipconfig /all >ipconfig.txt

4.   Now, open your Notepad to view the contents of the text file as follows.

>>> PS C:\> notepad ipconfig.txt

Now, entering a single command into PowerShell is helpful, but at some times you need more than a single command to provide troubleshooting configuration or information details to help with the setup related issues or the performance issues. This is where PowerShell is really shone on Windows. You would have had to either write a batch file in the past, or enter the commands manually. This is shown in the following script of TroubleShoot.bat.

Tshoot.bat ipconfig > C:\tshoot.txt route print > > C:\tshoot.txt hostname > > C:\tshoot.txt net statistics workstation > > C:\tshoot.txt Naturally, when you enter the commands manually, you have to wait for every command to be completed before entering the next command. In that case, you could always lose your place in the command sequence or wait for each command result.

Windows PowerShell does away with this issue. On a single line, you can now enter multiple commands, then leave your computer or start performing other tasks while the computer is produces the output. To achieve that capability, no batch file needs to be written.

Tip Use multiple commands over a single line of Windows PowerShell. Enter each complete command and separate the commands using a semicolon.

The following exercise describes how multiple commands can be executed.

1.   Now, open your Windows PowerShell by selecting Run and typing "PowerShell."

2.   Now, simply enter the ipconfig /all command. Pipeline the output to a text file is known as

<Tshoot.txt>

by the use of the redirection arrow, i.e., >. This would be the result.

>ipconfig /all >tshoot.txt

3.   On the similar line, just use a semicolon to separate all the command from the routed print command line. Now, just perpend your output from the commands to a file called "Tshoot.txt" by using the arrows ">>". Here is the command.

>>> ipconfig > > tshoot.txt;route print>>tshoot.txt

4.   Now, On the very similar line, you have to type a semicolon to separate the route print command from the hostname command-line. Additionally, perpend the output from the command-line to a simple text file, known as Tshoot.txt. The command is as follows now.

>>> ipconfig > > tshoot.txt ; route print >>tshoot.txt; hostname >>> tshoot .txt

5.   Now, on the similar line, we have to use a semicolon to separate the hostname command from the net statistics workstation command. Perpend the output from the command to a text file called Tshoot.txt by using the redirect-and-append arrow. The completed command looks like the following.

>>> ipconfig > > tshoot.txt; route print >>tshoot.txt; hostname

>>> tshoot .txt; net statistics workstation >>tshoot.txt

1.3 Security Threats while using the Windows PowerShell

As with any tool as versatile as PowerShell, there are some security concerns. Security, additionally, was one of the design destinations in the Windows PowerShell.

While launching Windows PowerShell, it executes in the user folder; this ensures you that you are in a unique directory where you will get permission to perform certain actions and activities. This is far safer than the opening at the root of the drive, or even opening in the rooted system.

The script running is by default, disabled and it may easily have managed through the Group Policies. It may also be managed on a per-session or basis per-user.

Controlling the Execution of Windows PowerShell commandlets

When you open a Command-line prompt, or entered a unique command to it, and execute it. You may find out what is it upto? What if the command helps you to Format the drive C:\? So, are you so sure to format your drive C? This section of the guide covers some of the parameters that may be supplied to the commandlets that provides you to control the manner that they may execute.

Not all the commandlets support all the parameters, most of them with the PowerShell do. The switch parameters you can use to control execution are suspending, -Confirm, and -WhatIf. Suspend parameter is not a switch parameter that you may supply to a commandlet, but rather, it's an action you may take at a confirmation command prompt and is, so, another method of controlling the program execution.

A Note to use:

WhatIf at a Windows PowerShell command-line prompt, enter the commandlets. Type the "-WhatIf" command to switch parameters after the commandlet. This only works for cmdlets that change the system configuration. Now, there is zero -WhatIf parameter for the cmdlets such as Get-Process that only displays information.

Here, windows PowerShell cmdlets that changes system states (such as Service), It supports a unique prototype mode such as you may enter by using the switching parameter. If the developer decides to implement the -WhatIf parameter when developing a cmdlet; here, the PowerShell team recommends that developers implement -WhatIf.

Confirming the actions

As you know that you can use -WhatIf to prototype a cmdlet in Windows PowerS hell. This is helpful in finding out what a commandlets does; Additionally, if you want to be prompted before the execution of the commandlet, you can use the "-Confirm parameter".

1.   Firstly, open the PowerShell, start and execute "Notepad.exe", you have to identify the procedure, and then examine your output.

2.   Now, you have to use "-Confirm parameter" to command-line prompt when using the Stop-Process commandlets to force stop the Notepad procedure to identify. Such as

>>> Stop-Process -id 3756 -confirm

The Stop-Process commandlets, when used along with "-Confirm parameter: shows the following line.

>>> Confirm: Are you so sure you want to end this process?

>>> Force stop operation "Stopping-Process" on Target "notepad".

>>> Yes [Y] Yes to All [A] No [N] No to All [L] Suspend [S] help [?]

3.   Now, you have to type "Y" and press "Enter". The Notepad.exe process will end. The PowerShell prompt returns to the default, ready for new commands, as shown here.

>>> PS C:\>

Suspending confirmation of cmdlets

The ability to prompt for confirming a cmdlet's execution is extremely useful and may at times be vital to help maintain a perfect system uptime level. You may find times when you enter a very long command, and then remember that you must first check on something else. You may be in the mid of stopping several processes, for example, but you need to view details about the processes to make sure you don't stop the wrong one. You can tell confirmation for such eventualities that you wish to suspend the execution of the command.

1. Open Windows PowerShell, start a Notepad.exe instance, identify the process, and examine the output, as in steps 1 through 4 in the exercise "Use -WhatIf to prototype a command" The output shown on my machine is as follows. Note that the process ID used by your Notepad.exe instance will, in all probability, be different from the one on my machine.

2. To stop the Notepad procedure identified by the Get-Process Note* command, use the-Confirm parameter to force a prompt when using the Stop-Process cmdlet. Here is an illustration.

Stop-Process-id 3576-confirm The Stop-Process cmdlet will display the following confirmation prompt when used with the Parameter-Confirm.

Confirm: Are you certain you want to take this action?

Perform "Stop-Process" operation on target "notepad (3576)." [Y] Yes [A] Yes to Everybody [N] No [L] No to All [S] Suspend?] Aid ("Y" is the default)

3. Input s to suspend Stop-Process cmdlet execution. And then there's a double-arrow prompt, as follows.

PS:

C:>>2. Use the Get-Process cmdlet to get a list of all processes running starting with letter n. The syntax is as it is.

Get-Trial n* 5. Upon entering an exit, return to the previous confirmation prompt.

Again, the prompt for confirmation appears as below.

Confirm: Are you certain you want to take this action?

Perform "Stop-" operation on target "notepad (3576)." [Y] Yes [A] Yes to Everybody [N] No [L] No to All [S] Suspend?] Aid ("Y" is the default)

6. Type "Y" and simply press the Enter key to stop the process at the Notepad. No further confirmation has been given. The prompt now displays the default PowerShell prompt for Windows, as shown here.

>>> PS C:/>

1.4 Working with Windows PowerShell This section details how to access and configure Windows PowerShell Console.

Accessing Windows PowerShell After installing Windows PowerShell on a down-level system, it becomes readily available for immediate use. Pressing the Windows key on the keyboard and pressing "R" to create a dialog box running — or using the mouse to select Start Run PowerShell all the time — will become time-consuming and tedious, though. (This isn't a big issue on Windows 10, where you can simply enter PowerShell on the Start screen menu.) On Windows 10, both I pin Windows PowerShell and Windows PowerShell ISE to both the Start screen and the Taskbar. I replace the CMD prompt with Windows PowerShell console on Windows Server 2012 R2, running Server Core. This is ideal for me and the way I work so I wrote a script to do it. This script may be called to automatically deploy the shortcut on the desktop through a log-on script. The script includes both the Windows PowerShell console and Windows PowerShell ISE to both the Start screen and Taskbar on Windows 10. On Windows 7, it adds to the taskbar as well as to the Start menu. The script only works for operating systems in the US English–language. To make it work in other programming languages, change the $pinToStart and $pinToTaskBar values to the target language equivalents.

Note:

> > > PinToStart.ps1

> >> $pinToStart= "Pin to Start"

> > > $file=@(Join-Path-Path $PSHOME-childpath "PowerShell.exe"), (Join-Path-Path $PSHOME-childpath "powershell ise.exe"))

> > > Foreach($f in $file)

> > > {$path= Split-Path $f > > $shell= New-Object-com "Shell. Application"

> > > $folder=$shell. Namespace($)

Configuring the Windows PowerShell Console

Many Windows PowerShell items can be configured. You can store those items in a PSConsole file. Use the Export-Console cmdlet to export the Console configuration file, as displayed here.

PS C:\ > Export-Console

The PSConsole file is nowsaved by default in the current directory, and has a.psc1 extension. You save the PSConsole file in XML format. Here is a generic console file.

<?Version of xml=."1.0 "encoding="utf-8"?>

< PSConsoleFile ConsoleSchemaVersion="1.0 ">

<   PSVersion>5.0.10224.0</PSVersion>   <PSnapIns/> </PSConsoleFile >

Options for starting Windows PowerShell

1. Start Windows PowerShell with the-NoLogo argument, without the banner. This can be seen here.

PowerShell-2. Start a special version of Windows PowerShell using the argument -Version. This can be seen here.

PowerShell-Release 3 3. Start Windows PowerShell using a specific configuration file by specifying the argument-PSConsoleFile, as below.

PowerShell -ps-console file with my.psc1 console 4. Start Windows PowerShell, execute a particular command and then exit using the -command argument. The command itself has to be prefixed with an ampersand (&) and put in braces. This can be seen here.

PowerShell-command "& {Get-Process}" Supply options for cmdlets One of Windows PowerShell's useful features is the standardization of syntax while working with cmdlets.

This greatly simplifies Windows PowerShell learning, and language building. Table 1-1 lists the parameters common to all. Keep in mind that some of those parameters cannot be implemented by some cmdlets. If these parameters are used, however, they will be interpreted for all cmdlets in the same way, because the Windows PowerShell engine itself interprets the parameters.

The Update-Help cmdlet is one of the first commands to run when you open Windows PowerShell for the first time. As for Windows PowerShell version 3, this is because Windows PowerShell does not include helping files with the products. This doesn't mean that no help presents itself— it does mean that it requires an additional download beyond simply displaying syntax.

A default Windows PowerShell 5.0 installation contains numerous modules varying from installation to installation, depending on the functions and roles selected for the operating system. In fact, there are far fewer modules and cmdlets in Windows PowerShell 5.0 installed on Windows 7 workstations than are available on a similar Windows 10 workstation. However, this doesn't mean that everything is chaos, because the essential Windows PowerShell cmdlets–the core cmdlets–remain unchanged from installation to installation. Since additional features and roles often install additional Windows PowerShell modules and cmdlets, the difference between installations is that.

Windows PowerShell's modular nature requires further consideration when you update the help. Simply running Update-Help does not update all loaded modules on a given system. In fact, some modules may not support updatable assistance at all — these generate an error when you try to update help. The easiest way to get all possible help updated is to use both the parameter -Module and the Parameter-Force switch. The Update Help command for all modules installed.

Update-Help -Module*-Force One way of updating help and not receiving a screen full of error messages is to run the Update-Help cmdlet and completely delete errors. This technique can be seen here.

Update-Help -Module*-Force-ea. 0 The problem with this approach is that you can never be sure that you've actually received updated assistance for everything you want to update. A better approach is to hide errors during the update process, but also to show errors after completion of the update. The advantage of this approach is being able to show cleaner errors. That technique is illustrated by the script UpdateHelpTrackErrors.ps1. The first thing the HelpTrackErrors.ps1 update script does is to empty the stack of errors by calling the clear method. Next it calls the module Update-Help with both the parameter -Module and the Parameter-Force switch. Furthermore, it uses the Parameter-Error Action (ea is an alias for this parameter) with a value of 0 (zero). A 0 value means errors are not shown when the command is running. The script ends by using a For loop to walk through the errors and display exceptions to the error. The full script for UpdateHelpTrackErrors.ps1 appears here.

UpdateHelpTrackErrors.ps1 $error. Clear) (Update-Help -Module*-Force-ea 0 For I= 0; I-lt $error. Count; I++) {"nerror I $error[$i].exception} When the UpdateHelpTrackErrrors script is running, a progress bar is displayed, indicating progress as the updated help files are updating.

You can also determine which modules are receiving updated help by using the-Verbose switch parameter to run the Update-Help cmdlet. Unfortunately, the output scrolls so fast when you do this, that it's hard to see what has actually been updated. Rediriging the verbose output to a text file to solve this problem. All modules try to update help in the command that follows. In a folder named fso off the root, the verbose messages redirect to a text file named updatedhelp.txt

Update-Help -module * -force -verbose 4>>c:\fso\updatedhelp.txt Windows PowerShell has a high degree of discoverability; that is, you can simply use Windows PowerShell to learn how to use it. Online help serves a significant role in helping with this discovery. The Windows PowerShell help system can be entered in multiple methods.

Use the Get-Help cmdlet below to learn about using Windows PowerShell.

Get-Help Get-Help This command will print help over the cmdlet Get-Help. Illustrate the output from this cmdlet here:

SYNOPSIS

Displays Information about the commands and concepts of Windows PowerShell.

NAME

>>> Get-Help

SYNTAX

>>>Get-Help [[-Name] <String>] [-Category <String[]>] [-Component <String[]>]

>>>[-Full] [-Functionality <String[]>] [-Path <String>] [-Role <String[]>]

>>> [<CommonParameters>]

>>> Get-Help [[-Name] <String>] [-Category <String[]>] [-Component <String[]>]

>>> [-Functionality <String[]>] [-Path <String>] [-Role <String[]>] -Detailed

>>> [<CommonParameters>]

>>>Get-Help [[-Name] <String>] [-Category <String[]>] [-Component <String[]>]

>>>[-Functionality <String[]>] [-Path <String>] [-Role <String[]>] -Examples

>>> [<CommonParameters>]

>>> Get-Help [[-Name] <String>] [-Category <String[]>] [-Component <String[]>]

>>> [-Functionality <String[]>] [-Path <String>] [-Role <String[]>] -Online

>>> [<CommonParameters>]

>>> Get-Help [[-Name] <String>] [-Category <String[]>] [-Component <String[]>]

>>> [-Functionality <String[]>] [-Path <String>] [-Role <String[]>] -Parameter

>>> <String> [<CommonParameters>]

>>> Get-Help [[-Name] <String>] [-Category <String[]>] [-Component >>> <String[]>]

>>> [-Functionality <String[]>] [-Path <String>] [-Role <String[]>] -ShowWindow

>>> [<CommonParameters>]

Get Help about the (Comparison Operator)

To get some help for a PowerShell provider, you have to type "Get-Help" followed by its provider's name. Such as, if you want to get help for the Certificate provider, type:

>> "<cmdlet-name> -?"

Certification

More than "Get-Help", you may also type the "help" or "man", which displays one screen of text at a time, or

>> "<cmdlet-name> -?"

Get-Help works only for some command-lines.

Get-Help is used to obtain the help content that it displays from the help files of your desktop. Without these files, Get-Help just displays the simple information about command-lines. Some of the Windows PowerShell modules possess their own help files. But, in PowerShell 3.0, some modules may show up with no help files.

1.4 Use the Update-Help cmdlet

You may also view the topics for help for PowerShell online in the Library, such as, TechNet. To obtain the online help or topics, simply, use the parameter. For example:

>>Get-Help

>>Get-Process -Online

You may read all of the topics at:

http://go.microsoft.com/fwlink/?LinkID=107116.

If you enter a unique word that does not appear in any topic, this displays a list that includes that word.

Firstly, look for help files in the set for PowerShell, then in the parent locale, and then in a fallback.

Beginning in PowerShell, if this command does not let you find any help in the locale, it looks for help topics in English before displaying auto-generated help or returning any error message.

Further Note

In the versions, such as, Windows PowerShell 3 and 4, Get-Help cannot find topics in the modules unless any module is imported into the executing session.

This was a known issue. To get the "About topics" in any module, importing the module, either by running a cmdlet in the module or by using the Import-Module cmdlet.

Chapter 2: Variables and Objects

PowerShell's variables and artifacts make life much simpler by maintaining knowledge in its natural form: artifacts. For typical shells, users spend much of their time only attempting to resuscitate education that the round has transferred from its natural way to plain text. Tools have developed to alleviate the strain of dealing with plain text, but the task is still considerably more complicated than it needs to be.

Since PowerShell builds on the. NET System of Microsoft, essential information comes in the form of objects. NET—information and available packages closely related to that information.

Let's say you want a list of the processes running on your system. Your command in other shells (such as tlist.exe or /bin/ps) produces a plain-text summary of the running processes on your machine. You submit it to work with that performance through a bevy of word processing tools— if you're lucky enough to have them available.

Get-Process cmdlet from PowerShell produces a list of the processes that run on your machine. Nevertheless, compared to other shells, these are a device of maximum fidelity. Objects Diagnostics. Process directly from the. NET Framework. The. NET Framework documentation defines them as artifacts that "[provide] the access to local and remote processes. it also enables you to start and stop local system processes." With those artifacts in hand, PowerShell makes it easy for you to access object properties and to access their functionality on those objects (such as stopping them, starting them).

2.1 Properties of an Item as a List

Problem

You have an object (e.g., an error record, a directory item, or a. NET object), and you want to show specific information about it in a list format.

Solution

Transfer the item into the Format-List cmdlet to show intricate details about an object.

For example, to show an error in list format, type the following commands: $currentError= $error[0] $currentError Format-List-Force

Discussion

Many commands by default show a summary view of their output in table format, such as the Get-Process cmdlet: PS > Get-Process PowerShell Handles NPM(K) WS(K) VM(M) CPU(s) Id ProcessName —- For displaying it, you can use the Format-List cmdlet: PS > Get-Process PowerShell Format-List* NounName: Process Name: PowerShell Handles: 443 VM: 192176128 WS: 52363264 PM: 47308800 NPM: 9996 Path: C:\WINDOWS\system32\WindowsPowerShell\v1.0\power shell.exe Company: Microsoft Corporation Processor: 4.921875 FileVersion: 6.0.6002.18139 (vistasp2 GDR These are Format-Table, Format-List, Format-Wide and Format-Custom cmdlets. The cmdlet Format-List takes input and shows information as a list on that input.

By default, in PowerShell's installation directory, PowerShell takes the list of properties to view from the*.format.ps1xml files.

You will only get some limited collections of parks in many situations: PS > Get-Process PowerShell Format-List I d: 2816 Handles: 431 CPU: Name: PowerShell I d: 5244 Handles: 665 CPU: 10.296875 Name: PowerShell to show all properties of the object, use Format-List*. When you type Format-List* but still don't get a list of the features of the object, then the purpose is specified in the*. For mat.ps1xml files, but the list command does not specify anything to view. Use Format-List -Power, instead.

One standard stumbling block in the formatting cmdlets of PowerShell comes from placing them in the center of a script or pipeline: PS > Get-Process PowerShell Format-List Sort Name out-line output: the object of type "Microsoft. PowerShell. Commands. Internal. Format. FormatEntryData" is not accurate or in the correct series. A user-specified "format-*" command that conflicts with the default formatting method probably causes it.

Within, the formatting commands of PowerShell create a new type of object: Microsoft. PowerShell. Commands. Internal. Format.*. Once these objects make it to the end of the pipeline, PowerShell can immediately send them to a cmdlet output: Out-Default, by default. These Out-* cmdlets presume that the objects arrive in a particular order, so doing something about the formatting commands output creates an output device error.

Try to avoid calling the formatting cmdlets in the middle of a script or pipeline to solve this problem. When you do this, the script production doesn't lend itself to object-based manipulation, so synonymous with PowerShell anymore.

If you want to use that formatted output directly, you should send the output as defined in Recipe 1.23 via the Out-String cmdlet, "Program: Check Formatted output for a pattern."

For more information on the Format-List cmdlet, select Format-List Get-Help.

Display the Properties of an Item as a Table

Problem

You have a collection of elements (e.g., error records, directory items, or objects with. NET), and you want to view descriptive information about them in a table format.

Solution

Transfer those items to Format-Table cmdlet to show summary information about a collection of objects. It is the default formatting method for PowerShell item sets and offers a variety of useful features.

To use PowerShell's default formatting, you should tap the output of a cmdlet (such as the Get-Process cmdlet) into the Format-Table cmdlet: Get-Process Format-Table to show unique properties (such as Name and WorkingSet) in table formatting, enter those property names as parameters in the Format-Table cmdlet: Get-Process Format-Table Name, WS just

To instruct PowerShell to format the table in t PowerShell describes WS as the WorkingSet Process Property alias: Get-Process Format-Table Name, WS-Auto to specify a custom column description (such as WorkingSet process in megabytes), provide the Format-Table cmdlet with a custom formatting expression: $fields= "Name," @ {Mark=" WS (MB); "Expression= {$.WS/1 mb}; Align=" Right"}= Get-Process Format-Table $fields-Auto Discontinued. These are Format-, Format-, Format-and Format-cmdlets.

The cmdlet Format-Table takes input and shows information as a table on that input. By default, in PowerShell's installation directory, PowerShell takes the list of properties to view from the*.format.ps1xml files. If you type Format-Table*, you can show all the properties of the objects, but this is rarely a useful view.

The-Auto Format-Table parameter is a helpful way to format the table automatically in the most straightforward way possible. It does, however, come at a cost. PowerShell needs to analyze every element in the incoming collection of items to find out the best table layout. It doesn't make a difference for small sets of objects, but it does for big games (such as a recursive directory listing). Without the -Auto parameter, the Format-Table cmdlet will be able to view items. With the -Auto flag, the cmdlet only shows results after all feedback.

The last example shows perhaps the most fascinating aspect of the Format-Table cmdlet: the ability to create entirely custom table columns. A custom table column is defined similarly to the way you define a custom column list. You can have a hashtable instead of defining an existing property of the products. The hashtable in-closes up to three keys: the mark of the column, an expression of formatting and alignment. The Format-Table cmdlet always shows the Label as the header for columns and uses the expression to produce data for that column. The mark must be a number, the expression must be a block of scripts, and the alignment should be either "left," "center," or "right." The $

(or $PSItem) the variable in the expression script block represents the individual formatted item.

The Select-Object cmdlet supports a similar hashtable but uses the name (rather than Label) as the key to defining the entity. Realizing how frustrating this was, PowerShell version 2 modified all cmdlets to accept both the Name and Tag.

The expression viewed in the last example takes the current element working package, dividing it by 1 megabyte (1 MB).

One standard stumbling block in the formatting cmdlets of PowerShell arises from placing them in the center of a script or pipeline: PS > Get-Process Format-Table Sort Name out-line output: the object of type "Microsoft. PowerShell. Commands. Internal. Format. FormatEntryData" is not right or in the appropriate series. A user-"format-*" command that conflicts with the default formatting method cause it.

Within, the formatting commands of PowerShell create a new type of object: Microsoft. Commands. PowerShell. Internal. Format.*. When these objects make it till the end of the pipeline, PowerShell will then automatically send them to a cmdlet output: Out-Default by default. These Out-* cmdlets presume that the objects arrive in a particular order, so doing something about the formatting commands output creates an output device error.

Try to avoid calling the formatting cmdlets in the middle of a script or pipeline to solve this problem. When you do this, the script production doesn't lend itself to object-manipulation so synonymous with PowerShell anymore.

If you want to make direct use of the formatted data, send the data through the Out-String cmdlet as described in Recipe 1.23, "Program: Search Formatted Output for a Pattern."

2.2 Store Information in Variables

Problem

You want to store the pipeline or command data for later use or to deal with it in greater detail.

Solution

Store commands data in a variable to save data for later use. This knowledge can be accessed later, or even transferred down the pipeline as if it were the initial command output: PS > $result= 2 + 2 PS > $result 4 PS > $output= IP config PS > $output Select-String "Default Gateway" Select-First 1 Default Gateway.   192.168.11.1   PS   > $processes=   Get-PS   > $processes. Count 85 PS > $processes Where-{$.ID-eq0} Handles   NPM(K)   PM(K)   WS(K)   VM(M)   CPU(s)   Id ProcessName −-0 0 0 Idle

Discussion

Variables in PowerShell (and all other scriptings A variable name starts with a dollar sign), ($and almost any character will follow. PowerShell has a specific meaning for a limited number of characters, and PowerShell offers a way to create variable names that can include these.

For more detail on the syntax and types of PowerShell variables, see "Variables" The output of any pipeline or command can be stored in a variable for later use. If this command generates simple data (such as a number or string), then the variable contains simple data. If the power produces rich data (such as the objects from the Get-Process cmdlet that represent machine processes), then the variable includes the collection of precious data. If the command (such as a conventional executable) produces plain text (such as the traditional executable output), then the plain text is in the variable.

When you have put a large amount of data into a variable but no longer need that data, assign a new value to that variable (such as $null). That will always allow PowerShell to release the memory that is used to store the data.

Besides the variables you make, PowerShell automatically specifies several variables that represent items like your profile file position, PowerShell's process ID, and more. Type Get-Help about automatic variables for a full list of such automatic variables.

2.3 Access Environment Variables

Problem

You want to use an environment variable in your script or interactive session (such as the device route or current user name).

Solution

PowerShell provides several ways to control variables in the system.

List the kids of the env drive to list all environment variables: Get-ChildItem env: To get an environment variable using a smaller syntax, use $env:$env: variable name to get an environment variable using its supply env: provider path, or environment: to Get-ChildItem cmdlet: Get-ChildItem env: variable name Get-ChildItem env: Providers allow you to deal as well with data stores (such as registry, environment variables, and aliases) as you would access the filesystem.

By default, PowerShell generates a drive (known as env) that works with the environment provider to allow you to access variables in the environment. You can access objects in the env through the environment provider: drive as you must any other drive: dir env:\variablename or dir env: variable name. You can also use dir Environment:: variable name if you want to access the provider directly (rather than going through its drive).

Nonetheless, typing $env: variable name is the most common (and easiest) way to deal with the Environment variables. It works for any provider but is most often associated with variables for the environment.

It is because the environment provider shares something with some other providers— namely supporting the core cmdlets* -Content package (see Example 3-1).

Excel 3-1. Working with content on various providers PS > "hello world" > test PS > Get-Content check hello world PS > Get-Content c: check hello world PS > Get-Content variable: ErrorActionPreference Continue PS > Get-Content function: more param([string[]]$paths) $OutputEncoding= [System. Console]::OutputEncoding if($paths){preach ($file in $paths) {Get-Content $file more.com.

E.g. 3-2. Use the special variable syntax of PowerShell to reach PS information > $function: more param([string[]]$paths);if($paths -ne $null) -and ($paths.length-ne 0))){...

Get $local: file Out-Host -p}} {$input Out-Host...

PS > $variable: ErrorActionPreference Continue PS > $c: test hello world PS > $env: systemroot C:\WINDOWS This variable syntax which is for content management helps you to both get and set information: PS > $function: more= {$input less.exe} PS > $function: more $input less.exe Now, as you use this approach to navigate complex provider routes, you can easily run into naming problems (eve}

At line:1 char:17 + $c:\temp\test.txt < < < < < PowerShell's escape support for complex variable names is the answer to that.

Enclose it in braces to describe a complex name variable: PS > ${1234123!@#$! #!@#$12Dollars!#####!"Type Mad!" PS > ${1234123!@#$! #!@#$12Dollars!#####!' feature!

The content equivalent (assuming the file exists) is as follows: PS > ${c:\temp\test.txt} Hello world since environment variable names do not contain special characters, this Get-Content variable syntax is the best (and easiest) way to access environment variables.

Program: hold on Changes to Environment Variables which Set by a Batch File

When a batch file changes an environment variable, cmd.exe maintains the modification even after exiting the script. It also creates problems, since one batch file will inadvertently pollute another's climate. It is said, batch file writers often deliberately adjust the global environment to modify the system's direction and other aspects to match a particular mission.

Environment variables, however, are private process information, which vanishes when the process exits. This makes the environment mentioned above configuration scripts stop running when you run them from PowerShell — just as they fail to work when you run them from another cmd.exe (e.g., MyEnvironmentCustomizer.cmd, cmd.exe/c).

The Example 3-3 script allows you to run batch files that alter the environment even after exiting cmd.exe and maintain their changes. It is done by storing the Environment variables in a text file until the batch file is through and then setting all the variables in your PowerShell session again.

Type Invoke-CmdScript Scriptname.cmd or Invoke-CmdScript Scriptname.bat to run this script —whatever extension the batch files use.

Whether this is the first time you run a PowerShell file, you'll need to customize your Execution Policy. See Recipe 18.1, "Allow Scripting Through an Implementation Policy," for more information on selecting an execution policy.

Notice that the full names for cmdlets are used in this script: Get-Content, Foreach-Object, Set-Content, and Remove-Element. It makes the writing accessible, which is suitable for texts to be interpreted by anyone else. Short aliases (such as GC, percent, sc, and RI) will make you more competitive for short scripts and interactive use.

E.g.   3-3.   Invoke-CmdScript.ps1 ### ##Invoke- CmdScript ####From Windows PowerShell Cookbook (O'Reilly)   ##by   Lee   Holmes (http:/www.leeholmes.com/guide) ### #################################< #.SYNOPSIS call on the specified batch file and parameters, but also p

.EXAMPLE PS > sort foo-that-sets-the-FOO-env-variable.cmd @set FOO=%* FOO echo set to% FOO%.

PS > $env: FOO PS > Invoke-CmdScript "foo-that-sets-the-FOO-env-variable.cmd" Set to Check C:\Temp > echo FOO.

Set to Check FOO.

PS > $env: FOO Check #> param (# #Path to execute [Parameter(Mandatory= $true)] [string] $Path, ##Arguments to [string] $ArgumentList) Set-StrictMode -Version 3 $tempFile= [IO.Path]::GetTempFileName) (# #Store cmd.exe performance. We also request the cmd.exe output ##the environment table after the batch file completes cmd / c" "$Path" "$argumentList & & set >" "$tempFile" ""# #Go through the temp file environment variables.

##Set variables for every of them in our local setting. Get-Content $tempFile | Foreach-Object {if($

-match   "^(.*?)=(.*)$")   {Set-Content   "env:\$($matches[1])" $matches[2] }} Delete $tempFile

2.4 Program: Creating a Dynamic Variable

Many concepts sound too tiny to warrant a whole new command or feature while dealing with variables and commands but the script's readability suffers without them.

Several instances where this is evident are date arithmetic (it becomes yesterday (Get-Date).AddDays(-1)) and profoundly nested variables (window title becomes $host. UI.RawUI.WindowTitle).

Throughout the Internet, there are creative approaches that use the debugging facilities of PowerShell to create a breakpoint that changes the value of a variable if you try to read from it. This approach, while unique, causes PowerShell to assume that any scripts depending on the variable are in debugging mode. Sadly, this prevents PowerShell from enabling in those scripts any essential performance optimization.

We could write our extensions to make these more comfortable to use, Get-Yesterday, Get-WindowTitle, and Set-WindowTitle sound too trivial to deserve their commands.

By expanding its PSVariable class, PowerShell allows you to define your types of variables, but that feature is primarily designed for developer scenarios, not scripting. Example 3-4 solves this dilemma by creating a new kind of variable (DynamicVariable) that supports dynamic script actions when you get or try to set the value of the variable.

E.g. 3-4. New-
##
##################################New-
####From Windows PowerShell Cookbook (O'Reilly) ##by
Lee Holmes (http:/www.leeholmes.com/guide)
##
##############################< #.SYNOPSIS
Creates a variable that supports actions which are scripted for
If(Test-Path variable:\$name) {Delete element
variable:\$name-Force} ##Set the current variable, along with
its getter and setter. SessionState. PSVariable. Set

2.5 Operating with. NET Framework

Problem

Objects You want to use one of the features that makes
PowerShell so powerful to communicate with it: its intrinsic
support for. NET objects.

Solution

PowerShell offers ways to access methods and properties
(static as well as an instance).

To set a static method on a class, place the name of the type in
square brackets, and then separate the name of the course
from the name of the process with two colons. Such as:
[ClassName]:: MethodName(parameter list) To call a method
on an object, place a dot between the variable representing
that object and the name of the way: $objectReference.
MethodName(parameter list) To retrieve a static property on a
class, place the ty The .NET Framework is a comprehensive
set of groups. That class represents a particular definition and
the features and details closely related to each category. We
are working with the. NET Framework is one aspect of
PowerShell, which brings a rev- solution into the management
shell environment.

A.NET Framework class example is a system. Diagnostics. Process — feature grouping that "provides access to local and remote processes and enables you to start and stop your system processes." Type and class words are also used interchangeably.

Classes include methods (which allow you to do operations) and properties (which enable you to access information).

The Get-Process cmdlet, for example, generates objects from the system. Diagnostics. Process, not a plain-text report like typical shells. It is credibly simple to manage these processes because they involve a vibrant mix of knowledge (properties) and operations (methods). You no longer need to search a text stream for a process's ID; you only can query the object directly!

PS > $process= Get-Process Notepad PS > $process. Id 3872 Static methods [ClassName]:: MethodName(parameter list). Some methods only refer to the definition by which class is defined. Retrieving all operating processes on a network, for example, refers to the general principle of processes, rather than a particular method. Methods that refer to the entire class/form are called static methods.

For example: PS > [System. Diagnostics. Process]:: GetProcessById(0) This particular function is done easier by the Get-Process cmdlet, but it shows the ability of PowerShell to call methods on the. NET classes. In the System. Diagnostics.

Process class, it calls the static GetProcess Byrd method to get the process with the 0 ID. This produces the following output: handles NPM(K) PM(K) WS(K) VM(M) CPU(s) Id ProcessName $objectReference. MethodName(parameter list) Many methods apply only to unique, measurable realizations (called instances) of a class.

An example of this will be to interrupt a process that operates on the machine, as opposed to the general process idea. If $objectReference refers to a particular System. Diagnostics. Process (for example, as output from the Get-Process cmdlet), you can call methods to start it, stop it, or wait until it exits. Methods that function upon class instances are called methods, of course.

The term object is sometimes used with the term case, interchangeably.

For instance: PS > $process= Get-Process Notepad PS > $process. WaitForExit) (stores the Notepad process in the variable $process. On that particular process, it then calls the WaitForEx it) (instance method to pause PowerShell until the process exits. To learn about the various sets of parameters (overloads) that a given method supports, type the name of that method without any parameters: PS > $now= Get-Date PS > $now. ToString OverloadDefinitions — — — — — — ToString) (string ToString) (string to string(System. IFormatProvider Provider) string ToString(string format, System. IFormatProvider Provider) string IFormama string Look at the output of the Trace-Command cmdlet in this case, with MemberResolution as the trace form (see Example 3-5).

E.g. 3-5. PS > Trace-Command MemberResolution {[System. Diagnostics. Process]::GetProcessById(0)} DEBUG: MemberResolution Information: 0: cache hit, calling mechanism: static System. Diagnostics. Process GetProcessById(int processId) DEBUG: MemberResolution Information: 0: mechanism conversion claim.

DEBUG: Data about MemberResolution: 0: Converting parameter "0" to "System. Int32."

DEBUG: Data about MemberResolution: 0: searching for potential references.

Handles PM(K) WS(K) NPM(K) VM(M) CPU(s) Id ProcessName — — — — — — — — — — — — — — — — — — — 0 0 0 12 0 Idle When you adapt a C #example from the Internet and PowerShell cannot locate a method used throughout the example, the method might have been added through a fairly uncommon technique called explicit interface use. If this is the case, before calling the process, you can cast the object to that interface: $sourceObject= 123 $result= ([IConvertible] $sourceObject).ToUint16($null) Static properties [ClassName]::PropertyName or: [ClassName]::PropertyName= value As with static methods, some properties refer only to the idea that the class reflects. For example, the system. DateTime class "represents a moment in time, usually represented as a date and time of day." It contains a Now static property that returns the current time: PS > [system.DateTime]::: Now Saturday, June 4, 2010, 4:57:20 PM This particular task is best done by the Get-Date cmdlet, but it signifies PowerShell's ability to access properties on .NET items.

Although they are fairly uncommon, some types do allow you to set the value of some static properties: the [system. Environment]::CurrentDirectory property, for example. This property reflects the current directory of the process— which is the startup directory of PowerShell, as opposed to the direction that you see in your prompt.

Instance properties $objectReference. PropertyName or: $objectReference. PropertyName= value Certain properties apply only to unique, measurable realizations (called instances) of a class, like instance methods. Like the general idea of days and hours, an example of this would be the day of an individual moment in time.

If $objectReference refers to a particular System. DateTime (for example, as provided by the Get-Date cmdlet or [System. Date Time]:: Now), you might want to retrieve the day of the week, day, or month. Properties that return information on a class's instances are called instance properties.

For example: PS > $today= Get-Date PS > $today. DayOfWeek Saturday The current date is stored in the $today variable. It then calls the instance property DayOf Week to obtain the day of the week for that particular day.

Create an Instance of a .NET Object

Problem

You want to construct an instance of a—the NET objects to communicate with its methods and properties.

Solution

To construct an instance of an object using the New-Object cmdlet.

To create an example of an object using its default constructor, use the New-cmdlet with the class name as it is the only parameter: PS > $generator= New-System. Random PS > $generator. NextDouble) (0.853699042859347 These parameters are supplied to the New-cmdlet to create an instance of an object which takes parameters for its build. In certain examples, such as system. Windows. Forms assembly, the class can reside in a separate library that is not loaded in PowerShell by default. In that case, you should first load the assembly containing the class: Add-Type-Assembly System. Windows.

Forms $image= New-Object System. Drawing. Bitmap source.gif $image. Save("source converted.jpg," "JPEG) "To build an object and use it concurrently (without saving it later), wrap that call to New-Object in parentheses: PS > (New-Object Net.

WebClient). Nevertheless, PowerShell supports much more of the. NET Framework than just the artifacts generated by its cmdlets. Those additional parts of the. NET Framework includes an immense amount of features that you can use in your scripts and general system management activities.

See Example 3-6 for an instance of a generic entity.

In using any of these classes, the first step is to construct a class instance. Then store that example in a variable, and then work on that instance with the methods and properties. You use the New-Object cmdlet to construct an instance of a class. The first parameter for the New-Object cmdlet is the name of the form, and the second parameter is the Constructor's list of arguments if any. The New-Object cmdlet supports type shortcuts from PowerShell, so you never need to use the full available class name. See "Type Shortcuts" for more detail on the style shortcuts

When working with .NET objects, a common pattern is to build them, set some properties, and then use them. The New-Object cmdlet property parameter helps you to combine these steps: $startInfo= New-Object Diagnostics. ProcessStartInfo -Property@{' Filename'=' powershell.exe';' WorkingDirectory'= $pshome;' Word'=' RunAs'} [Diagnostics. Process]:::Start($startInfo) Or even simpler via the built-in conversion of PowerShell type: $startInfo= [Diagnostics. ProcessStartInfo]@{'Filename] Assuming $byte is an array of bytes: PS > $memoryStream= New-Object System. IO.MemoryStream $bytes New-Object: Cannot locate the ".ctor" overload and the count of the argument: "11." At line:1 char:27 + $memoryStream= New-Object < < < < System. IO.MemoryStream $bytes To solve this, include an array containing the following list: PS > $parameters=; $bytes PS > $memoryStream= New-Object System.

IO.MemoryStream $parameters or: PS > $memoryStream= New-Object System. IO.MemoryStream @(,$bytes) Load types from other assembly PowerShell makes the most common types accessible by d. However, others are only accessible after you load the library that describes them (called the assembly). For a class, the MSDN documentation includes the assembly, which defines it. See Recipe 17.8, "Open a. NET SDK Library" for more detail on loading forms from another assembly.

A list of the classes in the .NET Framework that is most useful to system administrators sees Appendix F. See Recipe 3.13, "Learn About Types and Artifacts" for more detail about the features of a class supports.

For more on the New-Object cmdlet, click Get-Help New-Object. For more detail, click Get-Help Add-Type on the Add-Type cmdlet.

Chapter 3: Loops and Flow Control

When you start writing scripts or commands that communicate with unknown data, looping, and flow control concepts are becoming ever more relevant.

The looping statements and commands of PowerShell let you execute an operation (or collection of services) without having to repeat the authorities themselves. It involves doing something a specified number of times, storing each object in a group on, or operating before a specified situation occurs.

The flow control and comparison statements from PowerShell allow you to adapt your script or com- command to unknown data. They let you execute commands based on that data value, skip commands based on that data value, and more.

Looping and flow control statements together make the PowerShell toolbox more flexible.

3.1 Decisions with Comparison and Logical Operators

Problem

You want to compare specific data with other data and make a decision on that basis.

Solution

Use logical operators of PowerShell to compare data pieces and make decisions based on those pieces.

Comparison operators-eq, -ne, -ge, -gt,-in, -not in, -lt,-le, -like, -not like,-play, -not contains, -is,-is not Logical operators-and,-xor,-not For a thorough overview (and examples) of these operators see "Comparison Opera-tors" (page 879).

Logical discussion and comparison operators at PowerShell allow you to compare data pieces or check data for any situation. An operator either compares two data pieces (a binary operator) or checks one data piece (a unary operator). All comparison operators are binary operators, as are the most logical operators (they compare two pieces of data). The only unary logical operator is the-not operator, which returns the true/false equivalent to the data it is evaluating.

Comparison operators compare two pieces of the entire data and return a result that depends on the particular operator of the comparison. You would want to test, for example, whether a set has at least a certain number of elements: PS > (dir). Count-ge 4True or whether a string matches a given regular expression: PS > "Hello World" -match "H.*World" True Most comparison operators often adjust to the form of their input. For instance, when you apply them to simple data such as a string, the comparison operators-like and-match decide if the line fits the defined pattern. If you use them to a specific data set, the same comparison operators return all elements that match the design you have in that array.

The-play operator takes as their statement a regular expression. One of the more famous symbols of the regular expression is the character, $, which indicates the end of the line. However, figure $also represents the start of a PowerShell element! Place the string in single quotes instead of double-quotes. to prevent PowerShell from reading characters as language words or escape sequences: PS> "Hello World"-match "Hello" True PS> "Hello World"-match' Hello$' False By default, PowerShell's comparison operators are case-insensitive; To use case-sensitive variants, prefix them with c: -ceq,-cne,-age,-CGT,-cin,-clt, -clike, -cnotlike, -cmatch, -cnotmatch, -ccontains, -cnotcontains For a thorough overview of the comparison operators, their case-sensitive equivalents and how they respond to their input, see "Comparison Operators."

Logical operators combine true and false statements and return to a conclusion based on the logical operator in question. You may want to test, for example, if a string fits the wildcard pattern you have and is longer than a certain number of characters: PS > $data= "Hello World" PS > ($data-like"* llo W*")-and ($data. Length-gt 10) True PS > ($data-like"* llo W*")-and ($data. Length-gt 20) False Some of the comparison operators implement elements of the logical operator Since it is so common to use the opposite of a contrast (much alike). PowerShell offers contrast operators (such as -cnotlike) to save you from explicit use of the the-not operator.

See "Comparison Operators" (page 879) for a comprehensive overview of the individual logical operators.

The essence of how we write a script or order that adapts to its data and input is the comparison operators and logical operators (when combined with flow control statements).

For additional information on such sentences, see also "Conditional Sentences"

For more information on the operators in PowerShell, select Get-Help About Operators.

3.2 Script Flow Using Conditional Statements

Problem

The circumstances under which PowerShell executes commands, or parts of the script are to be managed.

Solution

Use if, else if, and other conditional statements from PowerShell to monitor the execution flow in your script.

For example: $temperature= 90if($temperature-le 0) {"Balmy Canadian Summer"} elseif($temperature-le 32) {"Freezing"} Elseif($temperature-le 50) {"Cold"}otherif($temperature-le 70)" {Warm}" "{Hot} "Discussion Conditional statements include the following: if statement Runs the following script block if its condition is eva PowerShell makes this very simple by allowing you to explicitly assign the effects of a conditional statement to a variable: $result= if(Get-Process -Name notepad) {"Running"} else {"Not running"}. This technique is similar to a ternary operator in other programming languages, or may form the basis of one if you want a more compact syntax.

to get more information and help about those flow control statements type Get-Help About Flow Control

3.3 Large Conditional Statements with Switches

Problem

You want to find a more natural or more compact way to represent a big if-else if-else conditional statement.

Solution

Using the switch statement of PowerShell to represent a broad, if-else, if another conditional statement more conveniently.

For instance: $temperature = 20 switch($temperature) {{ $ -lt 32}{ "Below Freezing;" break} 32 {"Exactly Freezing;" break }{ $ -le 50}{ "Cold;" break }{ $ -le 70}{ "Warm;" break {"Hot"}}} Discussion PowerShell's switch statement allows you to easily check its input against a broad range of comparisons.

The switch statement supports several options that allow us to configure how PowerShell compares the input against the conditions— such as with a wildcard, regular expression, or even an arbitrary script block.

Because scanning through the text in a file is such a tedious job, this is explicitly supported by PowerShell's switch comment. Such additions make the statements on PowerShell switches even more efficient than those in C and C++.

Think how to evaluate the SKU of the current operating system as a further example of the switch statement in practice. The script running on Windows 7, for example, is Ultimate? Windows Cluster Server Edition? The Get-CimInstance cmdlet lets us determine the operating system SKU, but it returns its outcome as a simple number. A switch statement helps you to map these numbers to their English equivalents on the basis of the official documentation on this site:

```
##############################################################
##############################################################
##############################################################
############################################

Get-OperatingSystemSku

##

##      From Windows PowerShell Cookbook (O'Reilly)

##      by Lee Holmes (http:/www.leeholmes.com/guide)

##

##############################################################
######################################

<#
```

SYNOPSIS

Gets the SKU information for the current operating system

EXAMPLE

PS > Get-OperatingSystemSku

Professional with Media Center

```powershell
#>
param($Sku =
(Get-CimInstance                                                Win32
OperatingSystem).OperatingSystemSku)
Set-StrictMode -Version 3
switch ($Sku)
{
0  { "An unknown product"; break; }
1  { "Ultimate"; break; }
2  { "Home Basic"; break; }
3  { "Home Premium"; break; }
4  { "Enterprise"; break; }
5  { "Home Basic N"; break; }
6  { "Business"; break; }
7  { "Server Standard"; break; }
8  { "Server Datacenter (full installation)"; break; }
9  { "Windows Small Business Server"; break; }
10 { "Server Enterprise (full installation)"; break; }
11 { "Starter"; break; }
12 { "Server Datacenter (core installation)"; break; }
13 { "Server Standard (core installation)"; break; }
14 { "Server Enterprise (core installation)"; break; }
15 { "Server Enterprise for Itanium-based Systems"; break; }
16 { "Business N"; break; }
17 { "Web Server (full installation)"; break; }
18 { "HPC Edition"; break; }
```

19 { "Windows Storage Server 2008 R2 Essentials"; break; }

20 { "Storage Server Express"; break; }

21 { "Storage Server Standard"; break; }

22 { "Storage Server Workgroup"; break; }

23   { "Storage Server Enterprise"; break; }

24   { "Windows Server 2008 for Windows Essential Server Solutions"; break; }

25   { "Small Business Server Premium"; break; }

26   { "Home Premium N"; break; }

27   { "Enterprise N"; break; }

28   { "Ultimate N"; break; }

29   { "Web Server (core installation)"; break; }

30   { "Windows Essential Business Server Management Server"; break; }

31   { "Windows Essential Business Server Security Server"; break;}

32   { "Windows Essential Business Server Messaging Server"; break; }

33   { "Server Foundation"; break; }

34   { "Windows Home Server 2011"; break; }

35   { "Windows Server 2008 without Hyper-V for Windows Essential Server Solutions"; break; }

36   { "Server Standard without Hyper-V"; break; }

37   { "Server Datacenter without Hyper-V (full installation)"; break; }

38   { "Server Enterprise without Hyper-V (full installation)"; break;}

39   {   "Server   Datacenter   without   Hyper-V   (core installation)"; break; }

40   { "Server Standard without Hyper-V (core installation)"; break;}

41   {   "Server   Enterprise   without   Hyper-V   (core installation)"; break; }

42   { "Microsoft Hyper-V Server"; break; }

43   { "Storage Server Express (core installation)"; break; }

44   { "Storage Server Standard (core installation)"; break; }

45   { "Storage Server Workgroup (core installation)"; break; }

46   { "Storage Server Enterprise (core installation)"; break; }

46   { "Storage Server Enterprise (core installation)"; break; }

47   { "Starter N"; break; }

48   { "Professional"; break; }

49   { "Professional N"; break; }

50   {   "Windows   Small   Business   Server   2011   Essentials"; break; }

51   { "Server For SB Solutions"; break; }

52   { "Server Solutions Premium"; break; }

53   { "Server Solutions Premium (core installation)"; break; }

54   { "Server For SB Solutions EM"; break; }

55   { "Server For SB Solutions EM"; break; }

56   { "Windows MultiPoint Server"; break; }

59   {   "Windows   Essential   Server   Solution   Management"; break; }

```
60      { "Windows Essential Server Solution Additional";
break; }

61      { "Windows Essential Server Solution Management
SVC"; break; }

62      { "Windows Essential Server Solution Additional SVC";
break; }

63      { "Small Business Server Premium (core installation)";
break; }

64      { "Server Hyper Core V"; break; }

72      { "Server Enterprise (evaluation installation)"; break; }

76      { "Windows MultiPoint Server Standard (full
installation)"; break; }

77      { "Windows MultiPoint Server Premium (full
installation)"; break; }

79      { "Server Standard (evaluation installation)"; break; }

80      { "Server Datacenter (evaluation installation)"; break; }

84      { "Enterprise N (evaluation installation)"; break; }

95      { "Storage Server Workgroup (evaluation installation)";
break; }

96      { "Storage Server Standard (evaluation installation)";
break; }

98      { "Windows 8 N"; break; }

99      { "Windows 8 China"; break; }

100 { "Windows 8 Single Language"; break; }

101 { "Windows 8"; break; }

103 { "Professional with Media Center"; break; }
default {"UNKNOWN: "+ $SKU }

}
```

Although used as a way to express broad conditional statements more cleanly, a switch statement operates much like an extensive sequence of if statements, as opposed to a large series of if-else reports. Given the pro-vide input, PowerShell tests the information against each of the switch statement comparisons. If the comparison evaluates to correct, then PowerShell executes the following script fragment. Unless there is a break statement in that script row, PowerShell will proceed to assess the following comparisons.

3.4 Replication of Operations with Loops

Problem

Operations You want to run the same code block more than once.

Solution

Use one of the looping statements of PowerShell (for, foreach, while, and do) or the Foreach-Object cmdlet of PowerShell to run more than once a command or script block. See "Looping Statements' ' (page 885) for a detailed summary of such looping statements. For example: for loops for ($counter= 1; $counter-le 10; $counter++) {"Loop number $counter"} foreach loop foreach($file in dir) {"File length:" + $file. Length} Foreach-Object cmdlet Get-ChildItem Foreach-Object {"File length:"+ $.Length} while looping $response= "while($response-ne" QUIT) "{$response= Read-Host" Type anything} "do.

Typically you use a for loop when you need an exact number of times to operate. Since it is so simple to use this way, it is sometimes called a loop count.

If you have a list of items, you usually use a for each loop and want to visit each item on that list. If you don't have the entire array in memory yet (as seen in the dir array from the for each example above), typically, the Foreach-Object cmdlet is a more robust alternative.

Unlike the for each loop, as created by PowerShell, the Foreach-Object cmdlet lets you process each item in the array. It is an essential distinction; asking PowerShell to collect a large command's entire output (such as Get-Content massive file.txt) in a for each loop will quickly pull the device downwards.

A useful shortcut to repeat a command-line operation is PS > 1.. 10 for each {"Running"} Running Working Working Working Working Working working just Like pipeline-oriented functions, the cmdlet Foreach-Object allows you to specify commands to be executed before looping, during looping, and after looping completes: PS > "a," "b," "c" Before running your script block, a while loop checks for this, while a do.. while loop checks for the condition after running your neighborhood. A do until the loop is just like a do-while loop, except when the state returns $true, instead of returning $false.

Chapter 4: Strings, Arrays, and Operators

There are two types of strings in Windows PowerShell: literal strings, and expanding strings. You use the expanding string in the DemoWhileLessThan.ps1 script, which is indicated by using a double quotation mark("). A string literal uses a single quote mark ('). Here, you will be displaying the name of the variable, and the value contained in the variable is displayed. This is the perfect location for showing off the expanding string. In an expanding string, when a line is evaluated, the value contained in a variable is shown to the screen. Consider the following code, as an example. The value 12 is assigned to variable $i. You then place I inside a pair of double quotation marks, making the string expand. When evaluating the line I is equal to I you get "12 is equal to 12," which is not very illuminating though true. This can be seen here.

>>> PS C:\> $i = 12

>>> PS C:\> "$i is equal to $i"

>>> 12 is equal to 12

>>> PS C:\>

4.1 Understanding the String Literals

What you probably want to do is to display both the variable's name and the value contained within it. You would have to use concatenation in VBScript. You have to use the string literals, as shown here, for this example.

>>> PS C:\>$i= 12 PS C:\ >'

>>> I is equal to'+ I

>>> I is equal to 12 PS C:\ >

If you want to use the expanding string advantage, you must delete the expanding string character for the first variable (escape the variable). You use the escape character here, which is backtick (or a serious accent character) for this purpose. This can be seen here.

>>> PS C:\ >$i= 15

>>>PS C:\ >'''

>>> I is equal to I

>>> I is equal to 15

>>> PS C:\ >

You use the expanding string in the DemoWhileLessThan.ps1 script to print the status message of the value of the I variable during each trip through the While loop. For the first I variable, you suppress the expanding nature of the expanding string, so you can tell which variable you're talking about. You adds the value of the I variable by one as soon as you have done this. You use the $i++ syntax to do this. This is exactly the same as the following.

>>> $i=$i+1

The advantage here is that the syntax for $i++ requires less typing. The script for DemoWhileLessThan.ps1 is outlined here.

DemoWhileLessThan.ps1 I=0 While I-lt 5)

>>> {''' I is equal to $i.

>>> This is less than 5" $i++}

>>> #end while I lt 5

If you run the DemoWhileLessThan.ps1 script, the following output is provided.

I amounts to 0. This is equivalent to less than $5 i. This is less than 2 dollars i. This is less than 3 dollars i. This is less than 4 dollars i. This is less than 5

PS C:\ > A handy example of using the While statement Now that you know how to use the While loop, let's look at the WhileReadLine.ps1 script. The first thing that you do is initialize the variableI and set it to 0. You then use the cmdlet Get-Content to read the contents of testfile.txt and store the contents in the variable $fileContents.

To loop through the content of the text file, use the While statement. You may do this as long as the value of the I variable is less than the line count in the text file or equal to that. The length property represents the number of lines in the Text file. Inside the script block, the content of the $fileContents variable is treated like an array (which it is), and the I variable is used to index the value of each line in the $fileContents variable into the array. You then increment by one the value of the I variable. The script WhileReadLine.ps1 appears here.

WhileReadLine.ps1 I= 0 $fileContents= Get-Content-path C:\fso\testfile.txt While I= $fileContents[$i] $i++}

4.2 Using special features of Windows PowerShell

If you think the script for WriteReadLine.ps1 is a bit difficult, note that it isn't really any harder than the version for VBScript. The difference is that you have resorted to using arrays to work with the content you have received from the cmdlet Get-Content. To work with the data, the VBScript version uses a FileSystemObject and a TextStreamObject.

In reality, to read the contents of the text file you would not need to use a script exactly like the WhileReadLine.ps1 script. That's because the Get-Content cmdlet automatically does this for you. All you really have to do is use Get-Content to display the contents of TestFile.txt. This command can be seen here.

Get-Content-path c:\fso\TestFile.txt The contents are automatically emitted to the screen because the results of the command are not stored in a variable. The Get-Content command can be further shortened by using the gc alias and omitting the name of the-Path parameter (which is the default). When you do this, you create a command similar to the following.

GC c:\fso\TestFile.txt Use a Get-Alias cmdlet with the -Definition parameter to find the available aliases for the Get-Content cmdlet. The cmdlet Get-Alias searches for aliases which have a definition matching Get-Content. Here's the command, with the output you receive.

PS C:\ > Get-Alias-Definition Get-Content

Command Type	Name	Definition
Cindy	Cat	Get-Content
Cindy	GC	Get-Content

This section has shown you can use the While statement also showed that looping activities in VBScript don't always require you to use the looping behavior in their Windows PowerShell equivalents, because some cmdlets display information automatically. Finally, it discussed how to find the aliases you often use for cmdlets.

4.3 Using the Do...While statement

When working with VBScript the Do While... Loop statement is often used. This section deals with some of the benefits of the similar Do... While statement in Windows PowerShell.

The script for DemoDoWhile.vbs illustrates the use of the statement Do... while in VBScript. The first thing you do is set the variable I to a value of 0. Then, you create an array. To do this, use the function Array, and assign numbers 1 through 5 to the ary of the variable. You then walk through the array of numbers using the Do While... Loop build. As long as the variable I value is less than the number 5, you'll display the variable I value. Then you increase the variable value and you loop back around.

The script for DemoDoWhile.vbs is outlined here.

>>> demodowhile.vbs

>>> I= 0 ary= Array(2,3,4,5,6)

>>> Do while I < 6 WScript.

>>> Echo ary(i) I= I + 1

Loop When running the DemoDoWhile.vbs script in Cscript at the prompt command, the numbers 1 through 5 are displayed on the prompt command.

You can accomplish the same with Windows PowerShell. The scriptsDemoDoWhile.ps1 and DemoDoWhile.vbs are essentially identical. The differences between these two scripts are due to the differences in syntax between VBScript and Windows PowerShell. The first thing that you do with the Windows PowerShell script is assign a value of 1 to the I variable.

You then create an array of numbers 1 through 5, and store the array in the variable $ary. To make this a bit easier you can use a shortcut in Windows PowerShell.

In Windows PowerShell arrays are actually fairly easy anyway. If you want to create an array, the variable simply needs to be assigned multiple pieces of data. To do this, each piece of data is separated by a comma. This can be seen here.

$aires= 1,2,3,4,5

4.4 Using Range Operator in Windows PowerShell

If you need to create an array with 32,000 numbers in it, typing each number and separating them all with commas would be impractical. In VBScript, to add the numbers to the array, you would need to use a For - Next loop. You can also write a loop in Windows PowerShell but the range operator is easier to use. To perform this task, you use a variable to hold the created array of numbers and enter the start and end number separated by two periods. This can be seen here.

>>> $ary= 1 - 5

Unfortunately for letters the range operator doesn't work. But there is no one or nothing to stop you from creating a range of numbers that represent each letter's ASCII value, and then casting it into a string later.

4.5 Operations Over an Array in Windows PowerShell

You are now ready for Windows PowerShell's Do - While loop. You use the declaration Do and you open a set of braces. You have a block of scripts inside those braces. The first thing that you do is to index it into the array.

The value of variable I is equal to 0, on your first pass through the array. Thus, the first element is displayed in the $ary array. You next increase by one the value of the variable $i. You're done with the block of scripts now, so look at the While statement.

The condition you examine is the value of the variable $i. You will continue to loop around as long as it's smaller than 5. As soon as the I value is no more than 5, you stop looping.

This can be seen here.

```
>>> I= 0 $ary= 1.. 5
>>> do {$ary[$i] $i++}
>>> while I-lt 5)
```

One thing to be aware of is that you are evaluating the value of I because it can be a bit confusing. You started out I at 0. In your array the first number was 1. But, in Windows PowerShell, the first element number in the array is always 0 (unlike VBScript, where arrays can start with 0 or 1). The While statement evaluates the value of the I variable and not the value contained in the array. Therefore, the number 5 is shown.

Casting Do - While to the ASCII values

The DemoDoWhile.ps1 script can be changed to show upper case letters A through Z. Initialize the I variable first, and set it to 0. You then create a number range from 65 up to 91. Those are the values of ASCII for capital letter A through capital letter Z. Then you start the statement Do and you open the block for your script. The script is identical to the preceding one to this point. Cast the integer to a char, to get letters from numbers. To do this, use the data type of the char and place it inside square brackets. This is then used to convert an integer to a letter of upper case. The code for displaying the upper case letter B of the ASCII value 66 would look the following.

```
>>> PS C:\ >[char]66
>>> B
```

Since you know that the $caps variable contains a number array from 65 to 91, and that the I variable holds numbers from 0 to 26, you index the $caps array, cast the integer into a char, and display the results as follows.

>>> [Char]$caps

>>> [$i]

Increase the value of I by one, close the script block, and enter the While statement where the value of I is checked to make sure it is less than 26. As long as $i's under 26, you're still looping around. The full script for DisplayCapitalLetters.ps1 appears here.

>>> DisplayCapitalLetters.ps1

>>> I= 0

>>> $caps= 65.. 91

>>> do {[char]$caps[$i] $i++}

>>> while I-lt 26)

This section explored the Do... While the Windows PowerShell construction was compared to a similar VBScript construction. In addition, it also examined the use of the range operator and casting.

4.6 Using the Do - Until statements in Windows PowerShell

Looping technology is an essential part of mastering. It happens everywhere, and should be a tool you can use without thinking about it. When you face a collection of items, an array, or another bundle of items, you need to know how to walk through the mess without resorting to research, panic, or hours of Internet searching. This section looks at the Do... Until construction.

Most scripts looping in the Microsoft Script Center Script Repository appear to be using Do - While. Typically, scripts using Do... Until... Loops are used to read through a text file (do something until the end of the stream) or to read through a record set of ActiveX Data Objects (ADO) (do something until the end of the file). As you will notice here, these coding conventions are not required and are not intended to constitute limitations. Often, you can do the same thing using any of the various looping constructions.

Comparing the Windows PowerShell Do - Until statement with VBScripts

Consider the DemoDoUntil.vbs script before getting too far into this topic. In this script the variable I is assigned a value of 0 first. You then create an array containing the numbers 1 through 5 in it. You will use the Do... until construction to walk through the array until the variable I value reaches 5. This script will continue to run until the variable I value equals 5. That's what a Do... until building does — it runs until a condition is met. The difference between Do... until and Do... when examined in the previous section is that Do... when a condition runs while it's true and Do... until a condition becomes true. In VBScript, this means that Do... until it always runs at least one time, because the condition is normally evaluated at the bottom of the loop, while Do... when evaluated at the top of the loop, and will therefore never run if the condition is not true. However, this is not true for Windows PowerShell, as this section will show later.

Inside this loop, on the first pass through the loop, you first display the value contained in array element 0. This is because you set the variable I value equal to 0 first. You then increment the variable I value by one and loop around until the value of I is equal to 5. The script for DemoDoUntil.vbs can be seen here.

>>> DemoDoUntil.vbs

\>>> I= 0

\>>> ary= array(1,2,3,4,5)

\>>> Do Up to I= 5 ary(i)

\>>> I = i+1

\>>> Loop

4.7 Using the Windows PowerShell Do statement

Windows PowerShell lets you write the same script. In the script DemoDoUntil.ps1, you set the value of the variable I to 0 first. You then create an array containing the numbers 1 through 5. That array is stored in the $ary variable. You then arrive at the building Do (do-until). You'll open a set of braces after the keyword Do. You use the I variable inside the braces to the index into the $ary array and to get back the value that is stored in the array's first element (element 0). You then increment by one the value of the I variable. You keep looping through the elements in the array until the I variable is equal to 5. You end the script at that time. This script resembles the script which was examined in the previous section of DemoDoWhile.ps1.

\>>> DemoDoUntil.ps1

\>>> I= 0

\>>> $ary= 1.. 5

\>>> Do {$ary[$i] I+ +}

\>>> Up to I-eq 5)

The Do - While and Do - Until Statements Execute Just Once

In VBScript, the code inside the loop would never execute if a Do - while Loop condition was never true.

In Windows PowerShell, the Do - While and Do - Will always run at least once until constructions. This may be an unexpected behavior and is something you should concentrate on. This is shown in script DoWhileAlwaysRuns.ps1. The script assigns the variable I to a value of 1 You print a message inside the script block for the Do... While loop, which states that you are inside the Do loop. The condition of the loop is "whereas the variable I is 5." As you can tell, the value of the variable I is 1. The value of the I variable will therefore never reach 5, because you are not increasing it. The script for DoWhileAlwaysRuns.ps1 is exhibited here.

>>> DoWhileAlwaysRuns.ps1

>>> I= 1

>>> Do {"do inside the do loop"}

>>> While I-eq 5)

>>> The text "inside the do loop" will be printed out once when you run the script.

The script for EndlessDoUntil.ps1 is identical to the script for DoWhileAlwaysRuns.ps1, except for a small detail. Rather than using Do... In the meantime, you are using Do... until. The remainder of the script is identical. The value of the variable I is 1, and you print the string inside the do loop in the script block for the Do... until loop. For each Do loop this line of code should execute once until the value of I is equal to 5. Because the I value is never raised to 5, the script will continue running.

The script EndlessDoUntil.ps1 appears here.

>>> EndlessDoUntil.ps1

>>> I= 1

>>> Do {"inside the do loop"}

>>> Until I-eq 5)

You should remember how to interrupt the running of the script before running the EndlessDoUntil.ps1 script. Hold the Ctrl key down, then press C (Ctrl+C). This is the same sequence of keystrokes that would break a runaway VBScript executed in the Cscript.

While statements can be used to Prevent the Unwanted Execution

If you have a situation where the block of scripts is not required to execute if the condition is not true, use the While statement. In an earlier section the use of While statement was examined. You have the same type of script, again. You assign 0 to the I variable, and instead of using a Do... You use the While statement, kind of construction. The condition that you are looking at is similar to the condition that you used for the other scripts (do something while $i's value is 5). You will display a string inside the script block which states that you are inside the While loop. The script WhileDoesNotRun.ps1 is listed here.

>>> WhileDoesNotRun.ps1

>>> I= 0

>>> While I-eq 5)

>>> {"Inside the While Loop"}

It may be a bit anticlimactic but go ahead and run the script WhileDoesNotRun.ps1. No output should display to the console.

The For statement

A For - Next loop is rather easy to create in VBScript. In DemoForLoop.vbs an example of a simple For - Next loop is shown.

Defining a variable to keep track of the count, indicating how far you're going to go, defining your action and making sure you specify the Next keyword. That is all there's to it. The DemoForLoop.vbs can be viewed here.

>>> DemoForLoop.vbs

>>> WScript.

>>> Echo I Next

>>> For

>>> I= 1 To 54.7

Use of the For Statement

You can achieve the same in PowerShell for Windows. The For loop structure in Windows PowerShell is similar to that of VBScript; the Windows PowerShell For loop construct is For (< init >; < condition >; < repeat >) {< statement list>}. Both start with the keyword For, both initialize the variable and both specify to what extent the loop will progress. One difference is that a For. Next loop in VBScript increases the counter variable automatically. The variable is not automatically incremented in Windows PowerShell; instead you add $i++ to one-time increment of the I variable. You'll display the value of the I variable inside the script block (braces). The script for DemoForLoop.ps1 can be viewed here.

>>> DemoForLoop.ps1

>>> For($i= 0; I-le 5; $i++)

>>> {' I equals'+ I}

Windows PowerShell For statements are very flexible and you can leave one or more of them out. In the script DemoForWithoutInitOrRepeat.ps1, you exclude the for statement first and last sections.

On the script's first line you set the variable I equal to 0. Next you come to the statement For. The I= 0 was inside the For statement in the DemoForLoop.ps1 script; here, you move it to the script's first line. The semicolon is still required, as it separates the statement's three sections. The I-le 5 condition portion is the same as for the previous script. The section on repeat, $i++, is not used.

You display the value of the variable in the For statement script section, and you also increment the value of I by one. Remember there are two types of strings on Windows PowerShell: expanding and literal. In this chapter earlier these two types of strings were examined. The script DemoForLoop.ps1 shows an example of a literal string— what is entered is what is shown. This can be seen here.

>>> ' I equals'+ I

An example of an expanding string is in the DemoForWithoutInitOrRepeat.ps1 script. The variable value is displayed-not the name of the variable itself. To suppress the nature of expanding string use the backtick character to escape the variable. You can avoid concatenating the string and the variable when using the expanding string this way, as you did in the script for DemoForLoop.ps1. This can be seen here.

>>> I is equal to I

Somewhere the value of I must be incremented. Because in the repeat section of the For statement, it was not incremented, you must be able to increase it inside the script block.

The script DemoForWithoutInitOrRepeat.ps1 appears here.

>>> DemoForWithoutInitOrRepeat.ps1

>>> I–0 For(,$i-le 5,)

>>> I is equal to I $i++}

>>> When running the script

DemoForWithoutInitOrRepeat.ps1, the displayed output resembles the output generated by DemoForLoop.ps1. You would not be able to tell that two thirds of the parameters were missing.

By looking at all the three sections of the For statement you can make your For statement into an infinite loop. As position holders you have to leave the semicolons. If you omit the For statement's three parts it will look like the following.

For;) (Even if you can create an endless loop with the ForEndlessLoop.ps1 script, you don't need to do this if you don't want to. You may be able to use an If statement to assess a condition and take action when the condition is met. If statements are covered in the section "Using the If statement," then later in this chapter. You display the value of the variable in the ForEndlessLoop.ps1 script and increment it by one. The semicolon is a representation of a new line. So, if you wanted to, you could write the For statement in three lines. This would be useful if you possess a very complex statement, as it would make reading the code easier. The ForEndlessLoop scripting block. Ps1 script could be written in different lines, and the semicolon could be excluded. This can be seen here.

ForEndlessLoop.ps1 for(;){$i;$i++} You are greeted with a long line of numbers when running the ForEndlessLoop.ps1 script. Press Ctrl+C inside Windows PowerShell prompt to break out of the endless loop.

You can say that working with Windows PowerShell is all about choices: how you want to work and what you want to be trying to do. The Windows PowerShell statement is very flexible, and perhaps one day you'll find just the problem waiting for the solution you've got.

4.8 Use of the Foreach Statement

The Foreach statement is similar to VBScript's ForEach, Next Construct. You have to create an array of five numbers, 1 through 5, in DemoForEachNext.vbs script. Then you use the For - Each - Next statements to make your way through the variable ary array. The variable I is used to iterate via the array elements. The ForEach block is entered so long as the collection or array contains at least one item. When entering the loop all statements are executed for the first element inside the loop. This means that the following command for each element in the array is executed in the DemoForEachNext.vbs script.

Wscript. Echo I as long as the collection or array contains more elements, the statements inside the loop continue to execute for each element. If the collection or array no longer contains elements, the loop will be exited, and execution will continue with the statement following the Next statement. This appears on DemoForEachNext.vbs.

>>> DemoForEachNext.vbs

>>> ary= Array(1,2,3,4,5)

The DemoForEachNext.vbs script works like the DemoForEach.ps1 script for each I In ary WScript. Echo I Next Wscript.echo "All done." You first develop an array that contains the numbers 1 through 5 in the DemoForEach.ps1 Windows PowerShell script, and then you store that array in the $ary variable. This can be seen here.

$ary= 1.. 5 Then use the Foreach statement to scroll through the $ary variable array. To keep an eye on your progress through the array use the I variable. Inside the block of scripts, you display each variable's value. The script forDemoForEach.ps1 is shown here.

>>> DemoForEach.ps1

>>> $ary= Foreach

>>> 1.. 5

>>> I in $ary)

>>> I

Use of the Foreach statement on the Windows PowerShell

The perfect thing about Windows PowerShell is that from inside the Windows PowerShell console you can use the Foreach statement too. This can be seen here.

>>> PS C:\ > $ary= 1.. 6

>>> PS C:\ >

>>> foreach($v in $ary)

>>> V

>>> 1 2 3 4 5 6

Ability to use Foreach statement from the inside of the Windows PowerShell console can give you excellent flexibility when interactive. Much of the work done on the Windows PowerShell console is, however, about using pipeline. The ForEach-Object cmdlet can be used when working with the pipeline. This cmdlet acts similarly to the Foreach statement but is intended to handle pipeline input. The difference is, you don't need to use an intermediate variable to hold the array contents. You can create and send that array across the pipeline. The other difference is; you don't need to create a variable for the enumerator to use. Instead, you use the automatic variable $ (which represents the current item on the pipeline). This can be seen here.

>>> PS C:\ > 1.. 5}

>>> {$1 2 3 4 5

>>> For Each Object

Exit the For - Each StatementSuppose you don't want all of the numbers in the array to work. In VBScript terms, a statement Exit For is done early to leave a ForEach... Loop. You must use an If statement to perform condition assessment. When the condition is fulfilled you are calling Exit For. You use an inline If statement in the DemoExitFor.vbs script to make that determination. For these kinds of things the inline syntax is more efficient than spreading the statement over three lines. You have to keep in mind about the inline If statement is that the final End If statement does not conclude with it. The script for.vbs on DemoExitFor is shown here.

>>> DemoExitFor.vbs

>>> ary= Array(1,2,3,4,5)

>>> For every I

>>> In ary If I= 3

>>> Exit For WScript. Echo

>>> I

>>> Next WScript.

>>> Echo "Statement after next"

4.9 Use of the Break statement in Windows PowerShell

In terms of Windows PowerShell, you use the Break declaration to leave the loop early. You use an If statement inside the script block to assess the value of the I variable. If you call the Break statement if it is equal to 3, and leave the loop. Here's this line of code.

>>> If($i-eq 3) {break}

The fullDemoBreakFor.ps1 script appears here.

>>> $ary= 1.. 5

>>> ForEach($i in $ary)

>>> {if($i-eq 3)

>>> {break}

>>> I

>>> "Statement following foreach loop"

When the script runsDemoBreakFor.ps1 it displays numbers 1 and 2. Then it leaves the Foreach loop and follows the Foreach loop to run the line of code. This can be seen here.

>>> 1 2 Declaration in for-each loop.

>>> Using the break statement

If you don't want to execute the line of code after the loop statement, use the exit statement instead of the Break statement. This is shown in the script for.ps1 on DemoExitFor.

>>> DemoExitFor.ps1

>>> $ary= 1.. 5

>>> ForEach($i in $ary)

>>> {if($i-eq 3)

>>> {exit}

>>> I

>>> "Statement following foreach loop"

When the script runs DemoExitFor.ps1, the code lines following the Foreach loop never executes or runs.

This is because the break statement ends the script (the exit command attempts to close the ISE in the Windows PowerShell ISE discussed in Chapter 8, "Using the Windows PowerShell ISE"). The results of running the DemoExitFor.ps1 script are shown here.

1 2 In VBScript, you could achieve the same by using the Wscript. Quit statement instead of Exit For. As with the script DemoExitFor.ps1, the script DemoQuitFor.vbs never reaches the line of code that follows the For... Each loop. That is shown here in DemoQuitFor.vbs.

>>> DemoQuitFor.vbs

>>> ary= Array(1,2,3,4,5)

>>> For Each

>>> I

>>> In ary

>>> If I= 3

>>> Then WScript. Quit WScript.

>>> Echo I Next WScript.

>>> Echo "Statement after Next"

The use of the Foreach statement is examined in this section. This is used when you don't know how many items a collection contains. It permits you to walk through the collection and to work individually with items from that collection. Additionally, it also examined two techniques for exiting a Foreach statement.

4.10 Using the If statement

The If... Then... End If statement is fairly straightforward in VBScript. There are many things to know:

Ø The statements of If and Then must be on the same line.

Ø The If... Then... End If statement must end with the End If statement.

Ø End If there are two words, then not one.

If... Then... End If statement is displayed in the

>>> DemoIf.vbs script.

>>> DemoIf.vbs

>>> a= 5

>>> If a= 5

>>> Then

>>> WScript.

>>> Echo "a equals 5"

>>> End

If there is no keyword in the Windows PowerShell version of the If... Then... End If statement, then there is no End If statement. Windows PowerShell If statements are more easy to type. However, this simplicity comes with some complexity. The condition which is assessed between a set of parentheses in the If statement. You check in the DemoIf.ps1 script to see if the variable $a is equal to 5. This can be seen here.

If ($a-eq 5) the code that is executed is positioned inside a script block when the condition is true. The DemoIf.ps1 script block is shown here.

$a is equal to 5'} The DemoIf.vbs script version of Windows PowerShell is a DemoIf.ps1 script.

DemoIf.ps1 $a= 5 If($a-eq 5){' $a equals 5'} The one thing that is different about the Windows PowerShell If the statement is the operators for comparison. The equivalent sign (=) in VBScript is used as an assignment operator. It is also used for comparison as an equal opportunities operator. On the first line of code, the value 5 is assigned to variable a. This uses an assignment of the equal sign. The If statement is used on the next line of code to find out if a value is equal to 5. The same sign is used as the equality operator on this line of code.

This can be seen here.

A= 5 If a= 5 Then the difference between an equality operator and an assignment operator is fairly easy to tell in simple examples such as this. However, in more complex scripts things might be confusing. By having special comparison operators, Windows PowerShell removes that confusion. One thing that could help is realizing that the main operators are two long letters. Here you'll find common comparison operators.

Operator	Description	Example	Result
-eq	Equals	$a = 5 ; $a -eq 4	False
-ne	Does not equal	$a = 5 ; $a -ne 4	True
-gt	Greater than	$a = 5 ; $a -gt 4	True
-ge	Greater than or equal to	$a = 5 ; $a -ge 5	True
-lt	Less than	$a = 5 ; $a -lt 5	False
-le	Less than or equal to	$a = 5 ; $a -le 5	True
-like	Wildcard comparison	$a = "This is Text" ; $a -like "Text"	False
-notlike	Wildcard comparison	$a = "This is Text" ; $a -notlike "Text"	True
-match	Regular expression comparison	$a = "This is Text" ; $a -match "Text"	True
-notmatch	Regular expression comparison	$a = "This is Text" ; $a -notmatch "Text$"	False

Using assignment and comparison operators

Any assignment of value in a condition block will be evaluated as on or true, and so the script will be executed. In this example, the value 1 is assigned to variable $b. In the If statement condition, you assign the variable $a to the value of 12. Any assignment evaluates to true, and executes the block of scripts.

>>> PS C:\ >$a= 1; If ($a= 12) {"its true"}

Sometimes, if the condition is true, you have to perform one action, and another if the condition is false. In VBScript, you use the Construction If... Else... End If. The Else clause goes into effect immediately after the first action if the condition is true. This is shown in script for DemoIfElse.vbs.

>>> DemoIfElse.vbs

>>> a= 4

>>> If

>>> a= 5

>>> Then WScript. Echo

>>> "equals 5"

>>> Else WScript. Echo

>>> "a is not equal to 5"

>>> End

If the syntax is not surprising in Windows PowerShell. After you close the If statement script block brace, you add the Else keyword and open a new script block to hold the alternative result. This is mentioned here.

>>> demlifelse.PS1

>>> $a= 4

>>> If ($a-eq 5)

>>> {' $a equals 5'}

>>> Else{' $a is not equal to 5'}

Things get confused with VB if you want to calculate multiple conditions and have multiple results. The Else If clause makes provision for the second result. The second condition requires evaluation. The Else If clause gets its own condition, which is followed by the keyword Then. Following the Then keyword, you will list the code you wish to execute. The Else keyword and an End If statement follow. This is displayed in script DemoIfElseIfElse.vbs.

>>> DemoIfElseIfElse.vbs

>>> a = 4

>>> If a = 5 Then

>>> WScript.Echo "a equals 5"

>>> ElseIf a = 3 Then

>>> WScript.Echo "a equals 3"

>>> Else

>>> WScript.Echo "a does not equal 3 or 5"

>>> End If

4.11 Evaluating multiple conditions

The DemoIfElseIfElse.ps1 script for Windows PowerShell is a little easier to understand because it avoids the statement End If. You use ElseIf for every condition you want to evaluate (be aware it's just a single word). You put the condition inside a couple of parentheses and open your block for the script. Here's the script on DemoIfElseIfElse.ps1.

>>> DemoIfElseIfElse.ps1

>>> $a= 4 If ($a-eq 5)

>>> {' $a is 5'}

>>> ElseIf ($a-eq 3)

>>> {' $a is equal to 3'}

>>> Else{' $a is not equal to 3 or 5'}

In this section, use of the If statement has been reviewed. Comparison operators were also covered, as were assignment operators.

The Switch Statement It is a best practice to generally avoid using either VBScript or Windows PowerShell build type ElseIf, because there is a better way to write the same code.

You'd use the Select Case statement in VBScript to evaluate a condition, and select one outcome from a group of potential statements. In the script DemoSelectCase.vbs the value of 2 is assigned to the variable a. The statement Select Case is used to assess the value of variable a. Here's the syntax.

Select Case Test Expression The evaluated test expression is variable a. Each of the various cases contains potential values for expression of the test. If the a variable value is equal to 1, then the Wscript. Echo code "a= 1" is executed. This can be seen here.

Case 1

WScript. Echo "a= 1" Each of the various cases is assessed in the same way. The expression Case Else is executed if none of the preceding expressions assess to true. The full script for DemoSelectCase.vbs appears here.

DemoSelectCase.vbs a= 2 Select

Case 1

>>> WScript.

>>> Echo "a= 1"

Case 2

>>> WScript.

>> Echo "a= 2"

Case 3

>>> WScript.

>>> Echo "a= 3"

Case Else WScript. Echo "unable to determine value of" End Select WScript. Echo "Statement after select case"

Using the Switch statement

There is no statement of a Select Case in Windows PowerShell. However, there is a statement about the Switch.

The Switch statement in Windows PowerShell language is the strongest statement. The basic Switch statement begins with the keyword switch, followed by the condition to be evaluated placed within a pair of parentheses. This can be seen here.

Switch ($a) Next, a block of scripts is used to mark the switch statement off the script block. Inside this block of outer scripts, you will find an internal block for executing scripts. Each condition to be evaluated begins with a value, followed by the execution part of the script if the value matches the condition. This can be seen here.

>>> 1 {' $a= 1'}

>>> 2 {' $a= 2'}

Defining the default condition

If no match is found in the block of the script and the default statement is not used, the switch statement will be executed and the line of code following the switch statement will be executed. The Default Statement performs a similar function to the Select Case Statement in Case Else. The Default Statement is displayed here.

>>> Default{' Unable to determine a value of $a'}

The full script for DemoSwitchCase.ps1 is shown here.

>>> DemoSwitchCase.ps1

>>> $a= 2 Switch

>>> ($a)

>>> {1{' $a= 1'}

>>> 2{' $a= 2'}

>>> 3{' $a= 3'}

>>> Default{' Unable to determine value of $a'}}'

>>> 'Statement after switch'

Understanding matching with the Switch statement

The first matching case is the one which is executed with the Select Case statement. The line following the Select Case statement is executed as soon as the commands gathers. In this Selection Case statement, if the condition matches multiple cases, only the first match in the list is executed. Matches are not executed from lower in the list. So make sure the most important code to execute is set highest in the Select Case order.

Order is not a major design concern with the Switch statement in Windows PowerShell. This is because, by default, every match will be executed from within the Switch statement. An example of this can be seen in the script.

>>> demswitchmultimatch.ps1

>>> $b= 2

>>> Switch()

>>> {1

>>> {' $b= 1'}

>>> 2{' $b= 2'}

>>> 2{' Second match of the $a variable'}

>>> 3{' $b= 3'}

>>> Default{' unable to determine the value of $a'}}'

Statement after switch' When the DemoSwitchMultiMatch.ps1 script runs, the second and third conditions will be matched, and their script blocks therefore be executed. The script for DemoSwitchMultiMatch.ps1 yields the output shown here.

$a= 2 Second match of the $a variable Statement after switch Evaluating any array If the array is stored in a DemoSelectCase.vbs Case.vbscript, an error of type-mismatch will be generated. This error can be seen here.

Microsoft VBScript Runtime Error: Mismatch type The Windows PowerShell Switch statement can handle a $a variable array without any change. The array can be seen here.

>>> $a= 2,3,5,1,77

>>> DemoSwitchArray.ps1

script is displayed here.

>>> DemoSwitchArray.ps1

>>> $a= 2,3,5,1,77

>>> Switch ($a)

>>> {1{' $a= 1'}

>>> 2{' $a= 2'}

>>> 3{' $a= 3'} Default

>>> {' Unable to determine the value of $a'}}'

>> 'Statement after switch'

Controlling matching behavior If you do not want the multimatch behavior of the Switching statement, you can use the Break statement to change behaviour.

The Switch statement will be exited when the first match occurs in the DemoSwitchArrayBreak.ps1 script, because each of the match condition script blocks contains the Break statement. This can be seen here.

1{' $a= 1'; break} 2{' $a= 2'; break}3{' $a= 3'; break} You are not required to include the Break statement with each condition; instead, you could only use it to exit the switch after matching a particular condition. Here's the full DemoSwitchArrayBreak.ps1 script.

DemoSwitchArrayBreak.ps1 $a= 2,3,5,1,77 Switch ($a) {1{' $a= 1'; break} 2{' $a= 2'; break} 3{' $a= 3'; break} Default{' unable to determine the value of $a'}}' Statement after switch' This section examined the use of the Windows PowerShell Switch statement. It also discussed the Switch statement's matching behavior and the use of Break.

Creating multiple folders: Step-by-step exercises in the first exercise, as you create 10 folders in the C:\mytempfolder directory, you will explore the use of constants, variables, concatenation, decision making and looping. This directory was formerly created. If you don't have this folder on your machine, you can either manually create it, or modify the following two exercises to use a folder on your machine. In this section, you'll modify the script in the second exercise to delete the 10 folders.

Creation of multiple folders using scripting to Windows PowerShell 1. Open PowerShell ISE on Windows.

2. Create a $intFolders variable and have it hold the value 10. The code for doing this is outlined here.

$intFolders= 10 Three. Create a variable which is called $intPad. Put nothing in that variable yet. That code is displayed here.

4. $intPad. Creates a variable called I and inserts the value 1 there. The code for doing this is outlined here.

And I= 1 5. To create a variable named strPrefix use the New-Variable commandlet. Use the commandlet's-value parameter to assign a testcase value to the variable. To make $strPrefix into a constant, use the -Option parameter. The code for doing this is outlined here.

New variable -Name strPrefix-TestFolder Value-Constant option 6. Start a Do... Until you make a statement. Include the script block opens brace. That code is displayed here.

Don't do {7. Begin a statement If... Else. The condition to assess is if the I variable is less than 10. Here's the code that does this.

When I-lt 10) 8. Open the If statement block for script. Assign the value0 to the $intPad variable. This can be seen here.

{$tpad= 9. To create a new folder, use the New-Item cmdlet. The new folder will be created in directory C:\mytempfolder. The new folder name will consist of thetestFolder $strPrefix constant, the number 0 from the $intPad variable, and the number contained in the I variable.

>>> Recent - Path

>>> c:\mytempfolder- Name

>>> $strPrefix$intPad$i-Type}

>>> 10.

>>> Add Clause Else. That code is displayed here.

>>> Other

11. The block Else script is the same as the block If script, except that it doesn't include the 0 in the name that comes from the $integer.

Copy the recent item code line from the If statement, and delete the variable $intPad from the Parameter-Name. Here's the revised line of code.

{New item-Path c:\mytempfolder-Name of directory $strPrefix$i-Type} 12. Increase variable I value by one. Use the double-plus symbol operator(++) to do this. Here's the code that does this.

$i+++$13. Close the Else clause script block, and add the Until statement. The condition Until it evaluates is whether the variable I is equal to the value contained in the variable $intFolders + 1. The reason why you add 1 to $intFolders is so that the script will actually create the same number of folders as the $intFolders variable does. Because this script uses a Do... until the loop and before entering the Until evaluation the value of I is incremented, the value of I is always 1 more than the number of folders created. That code is displayed here.

>>> To

>>> 14

>>> I-eq

>>> $intFolders+ 1).

>>> Save to < yourname >

>>> CreateMultipleFolders.ps1.

>>> Go ahead with your script.

In the directory C:\mytempfolder you should find 10 folders created. That concludes this exercise step by step.

The following exercise shows you how to delete multiple folders.

Chapter 5: Windows PowerShell scripting best practices

One of the great things about PowerShell 5.0 on Windows is that it's extremely flexible. However, this comes at the cost of readability, complexity, and supportiveness. The best practices outlined in this appendix will help minimize the effects of any of the pitfalls. Windows PowerShell is not always the best practice for interactive Windows PowerShell commands, it is both a command-line environment and a scripting environment. For the scripting environment the following best practices apply.

5.1 General script construction

This section looks at some general considerations for the overall construction of scripts. This includes the use of functions, modules, and other considerations.

Include certain functions in the scripts which are using them. Though an include file or dot-source can be used in a Windows PowerShell function, such an approach may become a nightmare. If you admit which function you want to use but don't know which script is on to it, you need to look (unless the function resides in a module that is stored at a known and specified destination). If the script provides the function you want but has other elements you don't want, it's hard to pick from the script file and choose them. In addition, when it comes to variable-naming conventions, you must be very careful, because you might end up with conflicting variable names. You don't have a portable script any more when using an include file. Your script has always to travel with the library of functions.

I use functions in my scripts because it makes them easier to read and maintain. If I were to store these functions in separate files and then dot-source them, neither of my two personal objectives of function use would really be met.

There is one other consideration: when a script references an external script that contains functions, there now exists a relationship that must not be disturbed. If, for instance, you decide you would like to update the function, you might not remember how many external scripts are calling this function and how it will affect their performance and operation. If there is only one script calling the function, the maintenance is easy. However, for only one script, just copy the silly thing into the script file itself and be done with the whole business.

5.2 Use full cmdlet names and full parameter names

There are several advantages to spelling out cmdlet names and avoiding the use of aliases in scripts. First of all, this makes your scripts nearly self-documenting and therefore much easier to read. Second, it makes the scripts resilient to alias changes by the user and more compatible with future versions of

Windows PowerShell. This is easy to do by using the IntelliSense feature of the Windows PowerShell ISE.

Understand the use of Aliases

There are three kinds of aliases in Windows PowerShell: compatibility aliases, canonical aliases, and user-defined aliases.

You can identify the compatibility aliases by using this command.

Get-childitem alias: | where-object {$_.options -notmatch "Readonly" }

The compatibility aliases are present in Windows PowerShell to provide an easier transition from older command shells. You can remove the compatibility aliases by deleting aliases that are not read-only. To do every time you start Windows PowerShell, add the following command to your Windows PowerShell profile.

Get-childitem alias: |

where-object {$_.options -notmatch "Readonly" } | remove-item

The canonical aliases were created specifically to make the Windows PowerShell cmdlets easier to use from within the Windows PowerShell console. Shortness of length and ease of typing were the primary driving factors in their creation. To find the canonical aliases, use this command.

Get-childitem alias: | where-object {$_.options -match "Readonly" }

If you must use an alias, only use canonical aliases in a script

You are reasonably safe in using the canonical aliases in a script; however, they make the script much harder to read. Also, because there are often several aliases for the same cmdlet, different users of Windows PowerShell might have their own personal favorite aliases. Additionally, because the canonical aliases are just read-only, even a canonical alias can be removed. However, worse than deleting an alias is changing its meaning.

Always use the description property when creating an alias

When adding aliases to your profile, you might want to specify the read-only or constant options. You should always include the description property for your personal aliases and make the description something that is relatively constant. Here is an example from my personal Windows PowerShell profile.

New-Alias -Name gh -Value Get-Help -Description "mred alias" New-Alias -Name ga -Value get-alias -Description "mred alias"

Use Get-Item to convert path strings to rich types

This is actually a pretty cool trick. When working with a listing of files, if you use the Get-Content cmdlet, you can only read each line and have it as a path to work with. If, however, you use Get-Item, you get an object with a corresponding number of both properties and methods to work with. Here's an example that illustrates this.

$files = Get-Content "filelist.txt" |

Get-Item $files |

Foreach-object { $_.Fullname }

General script readability

The following are points to keep in mind to promote the readability of your script:

- When creating an alias, include the -Description parameter, and use it when searching for your personal aliases. An example of this is shown here. (A better approach is to load the aliases from a private module. That way, the modulepath parameter also loads.)

Get-Alias |

where-object { $_.description -match 'mred' } |

Format-Table -Property " ",name, definition -autosize ` -hideTableHeaders

- Scripts should provide help. Use comment-based help to do this.

■ All procedures should begin with a brief comment describing what they do. This description should not describe the implementation details (how the procedure works), because these often change over time, resulting in unnecessary comment-maintenance work, or worse, erroneous comments. Place comments on individual lines—do not use inline comments.

■ Arguments passed to a function should be described when their purpose is not obvious and when the function expects the arguments to be in a specific range.

■ Return values for variables that are changed by a function should also be described at the

beginning of each function.

■ Every important variable declaration should include an inline comment describing the use of the variable, if the name of the variable is not obvious.

■ Variables and functions should be named clearly to ensure that inline comments are needed only for complex functions.

■ When creating a complex function with multiple code blocks, place an inline comment for each closing brace at the end of the closing brace.

■ At the beginning of your script, include an overview that describes the script, significant objects and cmdlets, and any unique requirements for the script.

■ When naming functions, use the verb-noun construction used by cmdlet names.

■ Scripts should use named parameters if they accept more than one argument. If a script only accepts a single argument, it is okay to use an unnamed (positional) argument.

- Always assume that users will copy your script and modify it to meet their needs. Place comments in the code to facilitate this process.

- Never assume the current path. Always use the full path, either via an environment variable or

an explicitly named path.

Format your Code

Screen space should be conserved as much as possible while still allowing code formatting to reflect logical structure and nesting. Here are a few suggestions:

- Indent standard nested blocks by at least two spaces.

- Block overview comments for a function by using the Windows PowerShell multiline comment feature.

- Block the highest-level statements, with each nested block indented an additional two spaces.

- Align the begin and end script block brackets. This will make it easier to follow the code flow.

- Avoid single-line statements. In addition to making it easier to follow the flow of the code, this also makes it easier when you end up searching for a missing brace.

- Break each pipelined object at the pipe. Leave all pipes on the right. Do this unless it is a very short, simple pipe statement.

- Avoid line continuation — using the backtick character (`). The exception is when not using line

continuation would cause the user to have to scroll to read the code or the output — generally around 90 characters. One way to avoid extremely long command lines for cmdlets with a large number of parameters is to use hash tables and splat parameters to Windows PowerShell cmdlets.

■ Scripts should follow Pascal-case guidelines for long variable names—the same as Windows PowerShell parameters.

■ Scripts should use the Write-Progress cmdlet if they take more than one or two seconds to run.

■ Consider supporting the -WhatIf and -Confirm switch parameters in your functions and in your scripts, especially if they will change system state. Following is an example that uses the -WhatIf switch parameter.

```
param(
    [switch]$whatif
    )
function funwhatif()
{
  "what if: Perform operation xxxxxx"
}
if($whatif)
{
  funwhatif #calls the funwhatif() function
}
```

■ If your script does not accept a variable set of arguments, check the value of $args.count and call the help function if the number is incorrect. Here is an example.

```
if($args.count -ge 0)
{
  "wrong number of arguments"
  Funhelp #calls the funhelp() function
}
```

■	If your script does not accept any arguments, use code such as the following.

If($args -ge 0) { funhelp }

Work with Functions

The following are points to keep in mind when working with your functions. They will make your code easier to read and understand:

■	Functions should handle mandatory parameter checking. To make this possible, use parameter property attributes.

■	Utility or shared functions should be placed in a module.

■	If you are writing a function library script, consider using feature and parameter variable names that incorporate a unique name to minimize the chances of conflict with other variables in the scripts that call them. It is best to store these function libraries in modules to facilitate sharing and use.

■	Consider supporting standard parameters when it makes sense for your script. The easiest way to do this is to implement cmdlet binding.

Create template files

The following are points to keep in mind when creating template files. You can create templates that can be used for different types of scripts. Some examples might be WMI scripts, ADSI scripts, and ADO scripts. You can then add these templates to the Windows PowerShell ISE as snippets by using the New-ISESnippet cmdlet. When you are creating your templates, consider the following:

■	Add in common functions that you would use on a regular basis.

■   Do not hard-code specific values that the connection strings might require, such as server names, input file paths, and output file paths. Instead, contain these values in variables.

■   Do not hard-code version information into the template.

■   Make sure you include comments where the template will require modification to be made functional.

■   You might want to turn your templates into code snippets to facilitate their usage.

Format Functions

When writing your own functions, you might want to consider the following:

■   Create highly specialized functions. Good functions do one thing well.

■   Make the function completely self-contained. Good functions should be portable.

■   Alphabetize the functions in your script if possible. This promotes readability and maintainability.

■   Give your functions descriptive names and follow a verb-noun naming convention. Nouns should be singular. If the function name becomes too long, create an alias for the function and store the alias in the same module as the function.

■   Every function should have a single output point (this does not include the error, verbose, or debug streams).

■   Every function should have a single entry point.

■   Use parameters to avoid problems with local and global variable scopes.

■ Implement the common parameters -Verbose, -Debug, -WhatIf, and -Confirm where appropriate to promote reusability.

Variables, Constants, and Naming

When creating variables and constants, and when naming them, there are some things to consider:

■ Avoid hard-coded numbers. When calling methods or functions, avoid hard-coding numeric literals. Instead, create a constant that is descriptive enough that someone reading the code would be able to figure out what it is supposed to do. In the ServiceDependencies.ps1 script, a portion of which follows, a number is used to offset the printout. This number is determined by the position of a certain character in the output. Rather than just writing "+14," a constant is created with a descriptive name. Refer to Chapter 12, "Remoting WMI," for more information. The applicable portion of the code is shown here.

```
New-Variable -Name c_padline -value 14 -option constant

Get-WmiObject -Class Win32_DependentService -computername $computer |

Foreach-object `

{

"=" * (((([wmi]$_.dependent).pathname).length + $c_padline)
```

■ Do not recycle variables. Recycled variables are referred to as unfocused variables. Variables should serve a single purpose; those that do are called focused variables.

■ Give variables descriptive names. Remember that you can use tab completion to simplify typing.

■ Minimize variable scope. If you are only going to use a variable in a function, declare it in the function.

■ When a constant is needed, use a read-only variable instead. Remember that constants cannot be deleted, nor can their values change.

■ Avoid hard-coding values into method calls or in the worker section of the script. Instead, place values into variables.

■ When possible, group your variables into a single section of each level of the script.

■ Avoid using Hungarian Notation, in which you embed type names into the variable names. Remember that everything in Windows PowerShell is basically an object, so there is no value in naming a variable $objWMI.

■ There are times when it makes sense to use the following: bln, int, dbl, err, dte, and str. This is due to the fact that Windows PowerShell is a strongly typed language. It just acts like it is not.

■ Scripts should avoid populating the global variable space. Instead, consider passing values to a

5.3 Function by Reference [ref].

Regular expressions quick reference

One of the really interesting features of Windows PowerShell is its ability to work with regular expressions. Regular expressions are optimized to manipulate text. Windows PowerShell uses regular expressions in many different places. Here is a listing of some of the places where regular expressions might be used:

■ Select-String cmdlet

■ ConvertFrom-String cmdlet

■ Where-Object cmdlet

■ Rename-Item cmdlet

- Switch statement

- Split statement

- Match operator

- NotMatch operator

- Replace operator

- Should object

Ordinary characters Characters other than . $ ^ { [(|) * + ? \ match themselves.

\a   Matches a bell (alarm) \u0007.

\b   Matches a backspace \u0008 if in a [] character class; in regular expression, it is a word boundary.

\t   Matches a tab \u0009.

\r   Matches a carriage return \u000D.

Character   Description

\v   Matches a vertical tab \u000B.

\f   Matches a form feed \u000C.

\n   Matches a new line \u000A.

\e   Matches an escape \u001B.

\040   Matches an ASCII character as octal (up to three digits); numbers with no leading zero are backreferences if they have only one digit or if they correspond to a capturing group number. For example, the character \040 represents a space.

\x20 Matches an ASCII character using hexadecimal representation (exactly two digits).

\cC   Matches an ASCII control character; for example, \cC is Ctrl+C.

\u0020   Matches a Unicode character using hexadecimal representation (exactly four digits).

The RegExTab.ps1 script illustrates using an escape sequence in a regular expression script. It opens a text file and looks for tab characters. The easiest way to work with regular expressions is to store the pattern in its own variable. This makes it easy to modify and even to experiment without worrying about breaking the script. (You simply use the # sign to comment out the line, and then you create a new line with the same name and a different value.)

In the RegExTab.ps1 script, "\t" is specified as the pattern. According to Table B-1, this means it is looking for tabs. The pattern, contained in $strPattern, is fed to the [regex] type accelerator, as shown here.

$regex = [regex]$strPattern

Next the content of the tabline.txt text file is stored into the $text variable by using the syntax shown here.

$text = ${C:\Chapter02\tabline.txt}

The matches method is then used to parse the text file and look for matches with the pattern that was specified in $strPattern. Notice that the pattern has already been associated with the regular expression object in the $regex variable. The script then counts the number of times it finds a match.

RegExTab.ps1

$strPattern = "\t"

$regex = [regex]$strPattern

$text = ${C:\Chapter02\tabline.txt}

$mc = $regex.matches($text)

$mc.count

Character   Description

[character_group]   Matches any character in the specified character group. For example, to specify all vowels, use [aeiou]. To specify all punctuation and decimal digit characters, use [\p{P}\d].

[^character_group] Matches any character not in the specified character group. For example, to specify all consonants, use [^aeiou]. To specify all characters except punctuation and decimal digit characters, use [^\p{P}\d].

[firstCharacter-lastCharacter]   Matches any character in a range of characters. For example, to specify the range of decimal digits from 0 through 9, the range of lowercase letters from a through f, and the range of uppercase letters from A through F, use [0-9a-fA-F].

.   Matches any character except \n. If modified by the Singleline option, a period character matches any character.

\p{name}   Matches any character in the Unicode general category or named block specified by name (for example, Ll, Nd, Z, IsGreek, and IsBoxDrawing).

\P{name}   Matches any character not in the Unicode general category or named block specified in name.

\w   Matches any word character. Equivalent to the Unicode general categories [\p{Ll}\p{Lu}\p{Lt}\p{Lo}\p{Nd}\p{Pc}\p{Lm}].   If ECMAScript-compliant behavior is specified with the ECMAScript option, \w is equivalent to [a-zA-Z_0-9].

\W   Matches any nonword character. Equivalent to the Unicode general categories [^\p{Ll}\p{Lu}\p{Lt}\p{Lo}\p{Nd}\p{Pc}\p{Lm}]. If ECMAScript-compliant behavior is specified with the ECMAScript option, \W is equivalent to [^a-zA-Z_0-9].

\s   Matches any white-space character. Equivalent to the escape sequences and Unicode general categories [\f\n\r\t\v\x85\p{Z}]. If ECMAScript-compliant behavior is specified with the ECMAScript option, \s is equivalent to [\f\n\r\t\v].

\S   Matches any non–white-space character. Equivalent to the escape sequences and Unicode general categories [^\f\n\r\t\v\x85\p{Z}]. If ECMAScript-compliant behavior is specified with the ECMAScript option, \S is equivalent to [^\f\n\r\t\v].

\d   Matches any decimal digit. Equivalent to \p{Nd} for Unicode and [0-9] for nonUnicode, ECMAScript behavior.

\D   Matches any nondigit character. Equivalent to \P{Nd} for Unicode and [^0-9] for non-Unicode, ECMAScript behavior.

Suppose you wanted to identify white space in a file. To do this, you could use the match pattern \s, which is listed in the above mentioned Table as a character pattern. The ability to find white space in a text file is actually quite useful, because for many items, the end-of-line separator is just white space. To illustrate working with white space, the RegWhiteSpace.ps1 script is shown at the end of this section.

On the first line of the script, a line of text to is created for testing against. The pattern comes from Table B-2 and is a simple \s, which tells the regular expression that you want to match on white space. The $matches variable is then used to hold the match object returned by the match static method of the regex type accelerator.

After the results of the match have been printed, you move to phase two, which is to replace, by using the same pattern. To do this, the pattern is fed to the replace method along with the variable containing the unadulterated text message. You then go ahead and print the value of $strReplace that now contains the modified object.

RegWhiteSpace.ps1

```
$strText = "a nice line of text. We will search for an expression"

$Pattern = "\s"

$matches = [regex]::match($strText, $pattern)

"Result of using the match method, we get the following:"

$matches

$strReplace = [regex]::replace($strText, $pattern, "_")

"Now we will replace, using the same pattern. We will use an underscore to replace the space between words:"
```

collections, looping through 167, 177 color of fonts, changing 333 columns 32, 36 -Columns parameter 28

COM-based objects 61, 62

CombinationFormatGetIPDemo.ps1 208 -Command argument 11 command lines, wrapping 350 -Command parameter 499 commandline property 350

command-line utilities 4-6, 19, 20, 22

commands

See also aliases; cmdlets building in Windows PowerShell ISE 260 copying to Clipboard 53 creating in Windows PowerShell ISE 274 editing in Windows PowerShell ISE 262 executing in parallel 549 finding 36–44, 53, 262 getting details of 36–44 listing history of used 338, 339 moving the insertion point 62 recursive 294

retrieving 336 running as different user 113 running as jobs 135 running from script pane 263 running from session history 339 running ipconfig 4, 5 running multiple 5 running on remote systems 135 running sequentially 559 running single 120–122 running via Commands add-on 262 setting breakpoints on 499–501, 509 Commands add-on 260, 264, 270–272 comments 593, 594 common classes 298

Common Information Model (CIM) cmdlets See CIM cmdlets -ComObject parameter 50, 51 comparison operators 169, 170 compatibility aliases 592 Complete-Transaction cmdlet 554 computer accounts, creating with ADSI

407, 408 computer connectivity 516, 546 computer names, creating an array of 133

-computer parameter 195

$computer variable 195

-ComputerName parameter 111, 112, 301, 347,

\e escape sequence 600 ea alias 143 See also - ErrorAction parameter

echo command 76 Else keyword 170 else statement 516 enabled property 447, 526

Enable-PSBreakpoint cmdlet 492, 554 Enable-PSRemoting cmdlet 114, 115, 135, 345 enabling QuickEdit mode 72 - Encoding parameter 329

EndlessDoUntil.ps1 161, 162

Enter-PSSession cmdlet 110, 118, 119, 132, 135,

439, 554 enumeration values 526 EnumNetworkDrives method

EnumNetworkDrives method 63 environment provider 104

and environment variables 77–79 Environment resource provider 565, 573 environment variables creating 78, 573 modifying 573–576 on computer, listing 335 removing 79 renaming 79 viewing new 575

$env:PSModulePath variable 230

-eq operator 169 -equals argument 310 error handling

adding 404 incorrect data types 532–536, 546 limiting choices 514–521 missing parameters 511–514 missing rights 521–523 missing WMI providers 523–532

Try...Catch...Finally 538–541, 545, 546 error stacks, clearing 534 -ErrorAction parameter 12, 13, 98,143, 144 errors

See also debugging Access Denied 295 capturing 539 creating objects 401–404 logic 478, 479 remote connections 112 remote procedure call (RPC) 342 run-time 474–478 scripts 143, 185 scripts, ignoring 295 suppressing messages 199 syntax 473, 474 system exceptions 199 trapping 199 WinRM (Windows Remote

Join-Path cmdlet 238, 295, 530

K

-Keep switch parameter 123, 128, 356

-key parameter 481

L

l attribute 413

LastWriteTime property 31, 60

LDAP

See also RDN (relative distinguished name) naming convention 399 provider 397

-le operator 169

Length property 31

-like operator 169 Limit-EventLog cmdlet 110 limiting choices 514

for parameter values 521 using -contains operator 517–521 using PromptForChoice 514, 515, 544, 545 using Test-Connection to identify computer

connectivity 516

-line parameter 492

List cmdlet 501

-list parameter 141, 298

-ListAvailable switch parameter 231, 234, 433

listing

aliases 107 environment variables 77 functions 86, 107 mapped drives 63 registry keys 91, 107 variables defined in a session 107

ListNamePathShare.ps1 script 322

Microsoft Management Console (MMC) renaming Active Directory sites 442 starting 399

Microsoft.PowerShellISE_profile.ps1 279

Microsoft.PowerShell_profile.ps1 279 -Minimum parameter 339 missing registry properties 98 missing rights 522 missing WMI providers

checking for installation 524–532 connecting to namespaces 523 information about 523

mkdir function 83.

Conclusion

Congratulations! If you've made it this far. We hope that you have truly begun to understand the basic concepts and complexities of Windows PowerShell. At this point, we suppose, you should be able to read almost any code written for Windows PowerShell with confidence and understanding.

We have tried to cover a fair number of important features of Windows PowerShell in this book, including some of the concepts of scripting programming languages. Furthermore, we have tried to make writing clear and easy to understand, and this book includes many theoretical, practical, and explained examples.

In the world of computer science and computer programming, you may find many academic books. Many of them are designed for students, and there you may find some other books which are purposely destined for the developers who need personal advice for how to resolve syntax problems and runtime problems, in the code, when developing a program. If you learn by coding, indeed, in this book, few pages do not have source code for Windows PowerShell, but every concept is demonstrated by at least one coding sample.

The code samples are very well-formatted, easy to read, and clean so that you may find the Windows PowerShell programming easy.

Moving forward, if you are a beginner in learning the Windows PowerShell, just read this book out as this book contains five chapters so that you may have a better understanding of the Windows PowerShell within a week.

Some people may say that this book is not for beginners! Just look at its size! This book is just too overwhelming for a beginner like you!

Don't listen to them!

You should go for an easier one if you find one. Well, we cannot tell you whether this book is right or wrong. We guess that everyone's understanding is quite different. We can suggest that this book is suitable for a person who is a noob in computer programming, but a business graduate!

References

- Guest. (n.d.). windows powershell 3 - PDF Free Download. Retrieved from https://vibdoc.com/windows-powershell-3.html

- Leonhard, W. (2020). Go pro: The power user's guide to PowerShell. Retrieved from https://www.infoworld.com/article/3126427/go-pro-the-power-users-guide-to-powershell.html

- Simple questions: What is PowerShell in Windows, and what you can do with it? | Digital Citizen. (2020). Retrieved from https://www.digitalcitizen.life/simple-questions-what-powershell-what-can-you-do-it

- Powershell Tutorial for Beginners: Learn in 1 Day. (2020). Retrieved from https://www.guru99.com/powershell-tutorial.html

- Powershell Tutorial - Tutorialspoint. (2020). Retrieved from https://www.tutorialspoint.com/powershell/index.htm

- Windows PowerShell Scripting Tutorial for Beginners. (2020). Retrieved from https://blog.netwrix.com/2018/02/21/windows-powershell-scripting-tutorial-for-beginners/

- PowerShell commands - PowerShell - SS64.com. (2020). Retrieved from https://ss64.com/ps/

- Wizard, P., Manager, P., & Powershell, T. (2020). Tips & Tricks You Need to Know About Windows Powershell. Retrieved from https://www.partitionwizard.com/partitionmanager/windows-powershell.html

- Windows PowerShell: Essentials. (2020). Retrieved from https://www.pluralsight.com/paths/windows-powershell-essentials

- What Is PowerShell? Webopedia Definition. (2020). Retrieved from https://www.webopedia.com/TERM/P/powershell.html

- Windows Powershell - CodeProject. (2020). Retrieved from https://www.codeproject.com/KB/powershell/

- Windows PowerShell Scripting and Toolmaking. (2020). Retrieved from https://www.globalknowledge.com/us-en/course/89827/windows-powershell-scripting-and-toolmaking/

www.ingramcontent.com/pod-product-compliance
Lightning Source LLC
Chambersburg PA
CBHW050537160726
48003CB00002B/648